Contents

99 Delicious Minestrone Soup Recipes: A Collection of Hearty Soups for Every Occasion

Munchie Mall Urus

INTRODUCTION

Welcome to 99 Delicious Minestrone Soup Recipes: A Collection of Hearty Soups for Every Occasion - your new go-to guide for flavorful Italian soups. Whether you're looking for a quick midweek meal, a comforting soup to share with your family, or a showstopping centerpiece for a special dinner party, you'll find it in this cookbook.

Made with just a few simple ingredients, minestrone soup is the perfect combination of hearty and nutritious. With 99 delicious recipes, you'll find plenty of tasty variations to suit any occasion. From a Classic Minestrone with Cannellini Beans to a vibrant Green Minestrone with Kale, each recipe is easy to make and guaranteed to please.

This cookbook starts with a comprehensive introduction to minestrone soup and the various ingredients you can enjoy in it. You'll also find helpful tips for ways to adapt the recipes to suit your own tastes and dietary needs. If you're a novice cook, there are plenty of tips and tricks for making cooking - even soup-making - simpler. And for those who are more experienced in the kitchen, there's plenty of creative ideas to play with.

You'll find all sorts of delicious soup recipes in the book, sure to please even the pickiest of eaters. There are vegetarian options with lots of vegetables, and recipes featuring beans, lentils, and other sources of plant-based protein. For non-vegetarians, there are recipes with chicken, beef, and Italian sausage. Some soups are more luxurious, such as the decadent Classic Italian Minestrone with Pancetta and White Wine.

There are also recipes for salads, breads, and other side dishes to complement your soup. Fans of Italian cuisine will appreciate all of the classic flavors and techniques in this collection. Every recipe includes easy-to-follow steps and beautiful photography.

With 99 Delicious Minestrone Soup Recipes: A Collection of Hearty Soups for Every Occasion, enjoy a hearty and delicious main course that's just a pot away. Get ready to whip up some classic minestrone soups, along with some new creations and twists. Enjoy your delicious minestrone soups and bon appétit!

1. Classic Minestrone Soup

Classic Minestrone Soup is full-flavored and hearty, with garden fresh vegetables and a sprinkle of parmesan cheese for a comforting and nourishing meal.

Serving: 6 | Preparation Time: 10 minutes | Ready Time: 45 minutes

Ingredients:
-2 tablespoons olive oil
-1 large onion, chopped
-1 large carrot, diced
-1 garlic clove, minced
-1/2 cup diced celery
-2 15-ounce cans of diced tomatoes
-1 15-ounce can of white beans, drained and rinsed
-4 cups vegetable broth
-2 cups water
-2 cups diced zucchini
-1 teaspoon Italian seasoning
-1/2 teaspoon salt
-1/4 teaspoon black pepper
-1 cup macaroni
-1/4 cup grated Parmesan cheese, for garnish

Instructions:
1. Heat the olive oil in a large soup pot over medium heat.
2. Add the onion, carrot, garlic and celery and cook, stirring occasionally, until the vegetables are softened, about 5 minutes.
3. Add the diced tomatoes and white beans and cook 1 minute more.
4. Stir in the vegetable broth, water, zucchini, Italian seasoning, salt, pepper and macaroni.
Bring to a boil then reduce the heat to a simmer.
5. Cook for 30 minutes, stirring occasionally, until the pasta is cooked and the soup has thickened.
6. Serve with a sprinkle of Parmesan cheese.

Nutrition Information:

Per serving: Calories 153, Total Fat 3.3 g, Saturated Fat 1.1 g, Trans Fat 0 g, Cholesterol 4 mg, Sodium 671 mg, Carbohydrate 26.8 g, Dietary Fiber 6.7 g, Protein 6.6 g

2. Vegetable Minestrone Soup

Vegetable Minestrone Soup is a deliciously hearty and wholesome vegetarian meal that combines a variety of different vegetables with the richness of a fragrant broth and flavor-loaded Red Kidney beans. This soup can be enjoyed all year round, and can be easily scaled up or down with ease.

Serving: 4-6 | Preparation Time: 15 minutes | Ready Time: 30 minutes

Ingredients:
-1/2 cup onion, diced
-1/2 cup carrots, diced
-1/2 cup celery, diced
-2 cloves garlic, minced
-1 tablespoon olive oil
-4 cups vegetable broth
-1 (14.5-ounce) can diced tomatoes
-1 (14.5-ounce) can red kidney beans
-2 cups cooked pasta, such as penne or shells
-1 cup frozen cut green beans
-1 teaspoon Italian-style seasoning
-Salt and pepper, to taste

Instructions:
1.In a large pot, heat the olive oil over medium heat.
2.Add the onion, carrots, celery, and garlic and sauté for 3 to 4 minutes.
3.Add the vegetable broth, tomatoes, red kidney beans, cooked pasta, and frozen green beans.
4.Bring the mixture to a boil, reduce heat to low, and simmer for 15 minutes or until all vegetables are cooked through.
5.Stir in the Italian-style seasoning, salt, and pepper.
6.Simmer for another 5 minutes.
7.Serve hot and enjoy!

Nutrition Information:
Serving Size – 1 cup, Calories – 150 kcal, Fat – 2.5 g, Carbohydrates – 23.5 g, Protein – 6.5 g, Fiber – 5 g, Sugar – 3 g, Sodium – 310 mg

3. Lentil Minestrone Soup

Lentil Minestrone Soup is a healthy, easy to make and delicious vegetarian soup that is packed with plant based proteins, flavorful and satisfying.

Serving: 4 | Preparation Time: 15 minutes | Ready Time: 45 minutes

Ingredients:
-1 tablespoon of olive oil
-1 yellow onion, diced
-3 cloves garlic, minced
-1 teaspoon of dried oregano
-1 teaspoon of dried thyme
-2 carrots, diced
-2 stalks of celery, diced
-1 zucchini (or other vegetable of your choice), diced
-1 cup of green lentils, soaked overnight
-6 cups of vegetable broth
-1 can diced tomatoes (14.5 ounces)
-2 tablespoons of tomato paste
-1 teaspoon of balsamic vinegar
-1 teaspoon of sea salt
-1 teaspoon of freshly ground black pepper

Instructions:
1. Heat the olive oil in a large pot on medium-high heat.
2. Add in the onion and garlic and sauté for about 5 minutes, or until fragrant.
3. Add in the oregano and thyme and stir for about 2 minutes.
4. Add in the carrots, celery, and zucchini and sauté for about 5 minutes.
5. Pour in the vegetable broth and add in the soaked lentils.

6. Bring to a boil and reduce to a simmer. Simmer for about 20 minutes, or until the lentils are tender.
7. Add in the diced tomatoes, tomato paste, balsamic vinegar, salt, and pepper. Simmer for an additional 10 minutes.
8. Serve hot with your favorite topping such as shredded cheese, croutons, sliced avocado, or fresh herbs.

Nutrition Information:
Each serving of Lentil Minestrone Soup contains approximately 300 calories, 11g of fat, 35g of carbohydrates, 13g of dietary fiber, and 11g of protein.

4. Italian Sausage Minestrone Soup

Italian Sausage Minestrone Soup is a hearty and flavorful soup that contains a delicious array of ingredients, including Italian sausage, carrots, celery, onions, and basil. This savory soup is sure to become a family favorite!

Serving: 8 | Preparation Time: 10 minutes | Ready Time: 50 minutes

Ingredients:
-1 lb Italian sausage
-2 tablespoons olive oil
-2 carrots, diced
-1 celery stalk, diced
-1 small onion, diced
-3 cloves garlic, minced
-4 cups chicken broth
-1/4 teaspoon freshly ground black pepper
-1 (14.5 ounce) can diced tomatoes
-2 (15 ounce) cans cannelini beans, rinsed and drained
-1/4 cup chopped fresh basil
-2 tablespoons chopped fresh parsley
-1 teaspoon salt
-1/2 teaspoon dried oregano

Instructions:

1. In a large pot, heat olive oil over medium-high heat. Add sausage and cook until browned, about 5 minutes.
2. Add carrots, celery, onion and garlic. Stir and cook until vegetables are tender, about 5 minutes.
3. Pour in chicken broth, black pepper, diced tomatoes, cannellini beans, basil, parsley, salt and oregano. Stir until combined.
4. Bring mixture to a boil. Reduce heat to medium-low and simmer for 35 minutes, stirring occasionally.
5. Serve and enjoy!

Nutrition Information:
Calories: 200, Fat: 8g, Carbohydrates: 18g, Protein: 12g, Cholesterol: 25mg, Sodium: 1020mg

5. Quinoa Minestrone Soup

With hearty vegetables, smoky bacon and a touch of Parmesan cheese, this quinoa minestrone soup is the perfect healthy and comforting meal.

Serving: Makes 6 servings | Preparation Time: 10 minutes | Ready Time: 40 minutes

Ingredients:
- 4 slices of bacon, cut into small pieces
- 1 onion, diced
- 2 cloves of garlic, minced
- 2 carrots, peeled and diced
- 2 celery stalks, diced
- 2 14.5 ounce cans of diced tomatoes
- 4 cups chicken broth
- 1 teaspoon dried oregano
- 1 cup uncooked quinoa
- 1 can cannellini beans, rinsed and drained
- 1 teaspoon salt
- 1/2 teaspoon freshly ground black pepper
- 2 tablespoons freshly grated Parmesan cheese

Instructions:
1. In a large saucepan, cook bacon over medium heat until crisp, about 5 minutes.
2. Add onion, garlic, carrots, and celery and cook until vegetables are softened, about 5 minutes.
3. Stir in tomatoes, broth, oregano, and quinoa and bring to a boil.
4. Reduce heat to medium-low and simmer for 20 minutes.
5. Add beans, salt, and pepper, and simmer for an additional 10 minutes.
6. Remove from heat and stir in Parmesan cheese. Serve hot.

Nutrition Information:
362 calories, 8g fat, 42g carbohydrates, 20g protein

6. Barley Minestrone Soup

Barley Minestrone Soup is a hearty and flavourful soup made with fresh vegetables, barley and other pantry staples. It's a great way to use up pantry staples and turn them into a nutritious and delicious meal.

Serving: 12 servings | Preparation Time: 20 minutes | Ready Time: 1 hour

Ingredients:
- 2 tablespoons olive oil
- 2 medium onions, chopped
- 2 cloves garlic, minced
- 2 medium carrots, diced
- 1 celery rib, diced
- 1 red bell pepper, diced
- 4 cups vegetable broth
- 2 cans (15 ounces each) diced tomatoes
- 1/2 cup pearl barley
- 1 can (15 ounces) red kidney beans, rinsed and drained
- 2 cups chopped kale
- Salt and pepper to taste

Instructions:
1. Heat the oil over medium heat in a large soup pot.

2. Add the onions, garlic, carrots, celery, and red pepper. Sauté until tender, about 5 minutes.

3. Add the broth, diced tomatoes, barley, and beans. Bring to a boil and reduce heat to a simmer. Simmer for about 20 minutes, until barley is tender.

4. Add the kale and season with salt and pepper. Simmer for 10 more minutes, or until vegetables are tender.

Nutrition Information:

Per serving: Calories: 172, Fat: 4g, Carbohydrates: 28g, Protein: 6g, Sodium: 579mg ·

7. Tuscan White Bean Minestrone Soup

This Tuscan White Bean Minestrone Soup is a comforting and hearty vegetable soup that is filled with delicious white beans and fresh veggies like spinach, carrots, and tomatoes. Perfect for a cold winter's night, this soup will make you feel right at home!

Serving: 8 | Preparation Time: 10 minutes | Ready Time: 40 minutes

Ingredients:
-4 garlic cloves, minced
-2 tablespoons olive oil
-1 onion, diced
-1 large carrot, diced
-3 ribs celery, diced
-4 cups vegetable broth
-1 (14.5-ounce) can diced tomatoes
-1 (14.5-ounce) can white kidney beans, drained and rinsed
-2 tablespoons tomato paste
-2 tablespoons chopped fresh basil
-1 teaspoon Italian seasoning
-2 cups baby spinach
-Salt and black pepper, to taste
-Grated parmesan cheese, for topping

Instructions:

1. In a large pot over medium heat, add olive oil and cook onion, carrot, and celery until softened, about 5 minutes.
2. Add garlic and cook for 1 minute.
3. Add vegetable broth, diced tomatoes, white beans, tomato paste, basil, and Italian seasoning. Bring to a boil.
4. Reduce heat, cover, and simmer for 20 minutes.
5. Add spinach, season with salt and pepper, and simmer until spinach is wilted, about 5 minutes.
6. Serve with grated parmesan cheese and extra black pepper, if desired.

Nutrition Information:
Cal. 137, Fat 5.8g (Sat: 0.8g), Chol.0mg, Sodium 545mg, Carb. 15.4g, Fiber 5.4g, Sugar 3.4g, Protein 6g.

8. Zucchini Minestrone Soup

Zucchini Minestrone Soup is a hearty and flavorful vegetarian soup that is packed with nutrition. With its combination of beans, vegetables, and pasta, it makes for a satisfying and nourishing meal.

Serving: 4-6 | Preparation Time: 10 minutes | Ready Time: 40 minutes

Ingredients:
- 2 tablespoons olive oil
- 1 onion, chopped
- 2 cloves of garlic, minced
- 2 carrots, peeled and chopped
- 2 stalks of celery, chopped
- 1 red pepper, chopped
- 4 cups vegetable broth
- 2 zucchini, chopped
- 1 15-ounce can white beans (cannellini, great northern, navy), drained and rinsed
- 1 teaspoon dried oregano
- 1 teaspoon dried basil
- 1 teaspoon smoked paprika
- 1 bay leaf
- 1/2 cup ditalini pasta

- Chopped fresh parsley and grated Parmesan cheese for garnish

Instructions:
1. Heat the olive oil in a large pot over medium heat.
Add the onion and garlic, and sauté for a few minutes until softened.
2. Add the carrot, celery, and red pepper, and stir to combine. Sauté for 3-4 minutes until vegetables are softened.
3. Pour in the vegetable broth, and bring to a simmer. Add the zucchini, beans, oregano, basil, smoked paprika, and bay leaf. Simmer for 20 minutes, stirring occasionally.
4. Add the ditalini pasta, stir to combine, and simmer for 12-15 minutes more, or until the pasta is tender.
5. Serve with optional garnishes of chopped fresh parsley and grated Parmesan cheese.

Nutrition Information:
Per serving (based on 6 servings): 242 Calories, 7g Fat, 37g Carbohydrates, 8.3g Fiber, 8.3g Protein.

9. Red Wine Minestrone Soup

Red Wine Minestrone Soup is an Italian soup that combines the delicious flavors of red wine, vegetables, beans and broth for an incredibly flavorful meal. Not only is this dish hearty and comforting, but it is also easy to prepare and can be ready in just a few hours!

Serving: 8 servings | Preparation Time: 15 minutes | Ready Time: 1 hour and 20 minutes

Ingredients:
- 2 tablespoons olive oil
- 1/2 cup onion, diced
- 2 cloves garlic, minced
- 2 cups canned or cooked beans (any variety)
- 1 cup carrots, diced
- 1 cup celery, diced
- 2 cups potatoes, diced
- 2 tablespoons tomato paste

- 2 tablespoons red wine
- 5 cups vegetable broth
- 1 teaspoon dried oregano
- 1 teaspoon dried basil
- 2 cups spinach, chopped
- 1/2 teaspoon salt
- 1/2 teaspoon black pepper

Instructions:
1. Heat the oil in a large pot over medium-high heat. Add the onion, garlic, carrots and celery, and cook until softened, 5-6 minutes.
2. Add the potatoes, tomato paste, red wine and vegetable broth. Bring to a simmer and cook until potatoes are tender, about 15 minutes.
3. Add the beans, oregano, basil, spinach, salt and pepper, and cook for an additional 5 minutes.
4. Taste and adjust seasoning as desired. Serve warm.

Nutrition Information:
Calories: 179 kcal; Fat: 4.5 g; Protein: 7.1 g; Carbs: 28.4 g; Fiber: 6 g; Sugar: 3.7 g

10. Roasted Vegetable Minestrone Soup

Roasted Vegetable Minestrone Soup is a hearty, savory dish that combines a delicious blend of roasted root vegetables with savory herbs and spices. This delicious soup makes for a perfect meal all year round!

Serving: 4 servings | Preparation Time: 15 minutes | Ready Time: 45 minutes

Ingredients:
- 3 cups of diced carrots
- 2 cups chopped onion
- 1 cup chopped celery
- 1 cup diced potatoes
- 4 cloves minced garlic
- 1 (14-ounce) can diced tomatoes
- 2 tablespoons olive oil

- 1 teaspoon thyme
- 1 teaspoon oregano
- 1 bay leaf
- 4 cups vegetable broth
- 2 cups cooked white cannellini beans
- 2 cups chopped kale
- Salt and pepper, to taste

Instructions:
1. Preheat the oven to 400 degrees F.
2. Place the carrots, onion, celery, potatoes, and garlic on a baking sheet. Drizzle with the olive oil, thyme, oregano, and bay leaf. Toss to combine. Roast in the preheated oven for 25 minutes, until golden and vegetables are tender.
3. Add the roasted vegetables to a large pot with the vegetable broth. Bring to a boil and then reduce to a simmer for 10 minutes.
4. Add the tomatoes, white beans, and kale to the pot. Simmer for an additional 10-15 minutes, until everything is heated through.
5. Season with salt and pepper, to taste. Serve warm.

Nutrition Information:
One serving of the Roasted Vegetable Minestrone Soup contains 180 calories, 10g of fat, 4g of protein, 20g of carbohydrates, 5g of fiber, and 130mg of sodium.

11. Spicy Minestrone Soup

If you're looking for a soup that is light but has a bit of a kick, this spicy minestrone soup is for you. With tomatoes, garlic and a hint of jalapeño, this is a meal that will warm your belly and please any crowd.

Serving: 6 | Preparation Time: 15 minutes | Ready Time: 45 minutes

Ingredients:
- 2 tablespoons olive oil
- 1 small yellow onion, chopped
- 4 cloves garlic, minced
- 1 jalapeño pepper, diced (remove seeds for less heat)

- 2 cans (14.5 ounces each) diced tomatoes with juice
- 4 cups vegetable broth
- 1 teaspoon freshly ground black pepper
- 1 teaspoon dried basil
- 2 zucchini, halved lengthwise and sliced
- 1 cup cooked small pasta, such as ditalini or mini shells
- 1 can (15 ounces) red kidney beans, rinsed and drained
- 2 cups chopped fresh spinach
- 1/4 cup chopped fresh parsley

Instructions:
1. Heat oil in a large stockpot over medium heat. Add onions, garlic, and jalapeño pepper, and sauté for 3 minutes.
2. Add canned tomatoes and juice, vegetable broth, black pepper, and dried basil. Stir to combine.
3. Bring soup to a low boil, reduce heat, and then cover and simmer for 15 minutes. Stir occasionally.
4. Add zucchini and pasta and then return to a low boil. Cover and simmer for an additional 15 minutes.
5. Add kidney beans, spinach and parsley, and then cook for 5 minutes more.
6. Serve warm with a drizzle of olive oil, freshly ground black pepper and/or grated Parmesan cheese.

Nutrition Information:
Servings Per Container: 6; Amount per serving; calories: 140; Total Fat 4g; Sodium 545mg; Total Carbohydrate 22g; Protein 5g.

12. Spinach Minestrone Soup

Spinach Minestrone Soup is a delicious and healthful vegetarian soup packed with savory flavors and nutrients.

Serving: 4-6 | Preparation Time: 10 minutes | Ready Time: 40 minutes

Ingredients:
- 2 tablespoons olive oil

- 1 large onion, diced
- 2 cloves garlic, minced
- 2 carrots, diced
- 2 stalks celery, diced
- 2 tablespoons tomato paste
- 6 cups vegetable broth
- 3 cans (14.5 ounces each) diced tomatoes
- 1 teaspoon dried basil
- 1 teaspoon dried oregano
- 1 teaspoon salt
- 1/4 teaspoon freshly ground black pepper
- 2 cans (15 ounces each) white beans, drained and rinsed
- 1/2 cup uncooked small pasta
- 4 cups fresh spinach leaves, chopped
- 1/4 cup freshly grated Parmesan cheese

Instructions:
1. Heat the olive oil in a large pot over medium heat.
2. Add the onion, garlic, carrots and celery and cook, stirring occasionally, until tender, about 8 minutes.
3. Add the tomato paste and cook, stirring constantly, for 1 minute.
4. Stir in the broth, tomatoes, basil, oregano, salt and pepper. Bring the mixture to a boil.
5. Reduce the heat to low and stir in the beans and pasta. Simmer for 25 minutes.
6. Add the spinach and cook for an additional 5 minutes.
7. Ladle the soup into bowls and sprinkle with the Parmesan cheese.

Nutrition Information:
Servings: 4-6, Calories: 241 kcal, Fat: 6.8g, Carbs: 33.6g, Protein: 11.2g

13. Farro Minestrone Soup

Farro Minestrone Soup is a comforting Italian-style vegetable soup featuring farro, a grain packed with fiber and protein. This delicious and hearty soup is easy to prepare, and it makes a satisfying meal on its own.

Serving: 6-8 | Preparation Time: 15 minutes | Ready Time: 40 minutes

Ingredients:
- 2 tablespoons olive oil
- 1 onion, diced
- 2 celery stalks, diced
- 2 carrots, diced
- 2 garlic cloves, minced
- 10 cups vegetable broth
- 2 teaspoons Italian seasoning
- 2 cups cooked farro
- 1 can (14.5 ounces) diced tomatoes
- 2 cups chopped kale
- 2 cups canned white beans, rinsed
- Salt and pepper, to taste

Instructions:
1. Heat the oil over medium heat in a large pot. Add the onion, celery, carrots, and garlic and cook, stirring often, until softened, about 5 minutes.
2. Pour in the vegetable broth, Italian seasoning, cooked farro and diced tomatoes. Simmer for 20 minutes.
3. Stir in the kale and white beans and simmer for an additional 10 minutes.
4. Season with salt and pepper, to taste.

Nutrition Information:
Calories: 262 kcal, Carbohydrates: 44g, Protein: 11g, Fat: 5g, Fiber: 8g

14. Kale and White Bean Minestrone Soup

Kale and White Bean Minestrone Soup is a healthy, comforting and comforting soup that is packed with nutritious flavors and textures. This soup is ideal for a quick and easy weeknight dinner or lunch and can be easily made in under an hour.

Serving: 4-6 people | Preparation Time: 15 minutes | Ready Time: 45 minutes.

Ingredients:
- 2 tablespoons olive oil
- 1 cup diced onion
- 2 cloves garlic, minced
- 3 large carrots, diced
- 1 stalk of celery, diced
- 6 cups of vegetable broth
- 2 cups diced potatoes
- 3 cups baby kale
- 1 (14.5 ounce) can white beans, drained and rinsed
- 1/2 teaspoon dried oregano
- 1/2 teaspoon dried thyme
- Salt & Pepper to taste

Instructions:
1. Heat the olive oil in a large soup pot over medium heat. Add the diced onion and garlic and cook until lightly browned, about 5 minutes.
2. Add the diced carrots and celery and cook for another 5 minutes.
3. Pour in the vegetable broth and add the diced potatoes. Bring the soup to a low boil and then reduce the heat to a simmer. Simmer for 15 minutes.
4. Add the baby kale, white beans, dried oregano, and dried thyme, and season with salt & pepper to taste. Simmer for another 15 minutes.
5. Serve the minestrone soup warm, garnished with fresh parsley or grated Parmesan cheese.

Nutrition Information (per serving):
Calories: 163, Fat: 5g, Saturated Fat: 1g, Cholesterol: 0mg, Sodium: 578mg, Carbohydrates: 23g, Fiber: 6g, Sugar: 4g, Protein: 8g

15. Sweet Potato Minestrone Soup

Sweet Potato Minestrone Soup is a hearty, rich soup, perfect for chilly days. It's packed with goodness, and is wonderfully filling.

Serving: 4-6 | Preparation Time: 15 minutes | Ready Time: 25 minutes

Ingredients:

- 2 tablespoons olive oil
- 2 onions, finely chopped
- 2 celery sticks, finely chopped
- 2 carrots, peeled and finely chopped
- 2 garlic cloves, crushed
- 2 sweet potatoes, coarsely chopped
- 400 g can haricot beans
- 1L chicken or vegetable stock
- 1/2 handful fresh basil leaves
- Salt and freshly ground black pepper

Instructions:
1. Heat the olive oil in a large heavy-based saucepan.
2. Add the onion and celery, and cook for 5 minutes until softened.
3. Add the carrots and garlic and cook for a further 3 minutes.
4. Add the sweet potatoes, haricot beans and stock, and simmer for 10 minutes or until the vegetables have softened.
5. Add the basil leaves, season to taste with salt and pepper.
6. Ladle into bowls to serve.

Nutrition Information:
Calories: 194; Total Fat: 5.5g; Cholesterol: 0mg; Sodium: 533mg; Carbohydrates: 30.3g; Dietary Fiber: 8.1g; Sugar: 5.1g; Protein: 6.6g

16. Chickpea Minestrone Soup

Chickpea Minestrone Soup is a hearty and nutritious soup that makes for the perfect comfort food. It is packed with flavour from the tomatoes, garlic, and onion, while being given a unique texture from the combination of diced vegetables, chickpeas and diced potatoes.

Serving: 4 | Preparation Time: 10 minutes | Ready Time: 45 minutes

Ingredients:
- 2 tablespoons olive oil
- 2 large garlic cloves, minced
- 1 small onion, diced
- 1 large carrot, diced

- 1 large celery stalks, diced
- 1 teaspoon dried thyme
- 1 (14.5-ounce) can diced tomatoes
- 1 small Yukon gold potatoes, diced
- 3 cups vegetable broth
- 2 (14.5-ounce) cans chickpeas, drained and rinsed
- sea salt and black pepper to taste

Instructions:
1. Heat the olive oil in a large pot over medium heat.
2. Add garlic, onion and carrots and sauté for about 5 minutes, stirring occasionally.
3. Add the celery and thyme and cook for another 5 minutes.
4. Add the tomatoes, potatoes, vegetable broth and chickpeas.
5. Bring to a low boil, cover and simmer for 30-35 minutes.
6. Add salt and black pepper to taste.
7. Serve warm.

Nutrition Information:
Per serving:calories: 306, fat: 7 g, carbohydrates: 49 g, protein: 14 g, sodium: 922 mg Dietary fiber: 11 g, sugar: 6 g.

17. Mushroom and Leek Minestrone Soup

Mushroom and Leek Minestrone Soup is a rich and flavorful combination of savory vegetables, beans and mushrooms. Packed with fiber and proteins, this soup is a great way to get cozy during winter days.

Serving: 4 | Preparation Time: 20 minutes | Ready Time: 45 minutes

Ingredients:
- 2 tablespoons olive oil
- 1 large onion, finely chopped
- 2 leeks, trimmed and finely chopped
- 2 cloves garlic, finely chopped
- 8 ounces white mushrooms, sliced
- 2 (14-ounce) cans vegetable broth
- 2 carrots, diced

- 2 potatoes, diced
- 2 stalks celery, diced
- 1 (14-ounce) can diced tomatoes
- 2 cups cooked white beans or a 15-ounce can of white beans, rinsed and drained
- 1 teaspoon dried oregano
- 1/2 teaspoon dried thyme
- 1/4 teaspoon red pepper flakes
- 2 tablespoons chopped fresh parsley
- 2 tablespoons chopped fresh basil
- Salt and black pepper, to taste

Instructions:

1. Heat the olive oil in a large pot over medium heat. Add the onion, leeks and garlic and cook, stirring occasionally, for 5 minutes, until the vegetables are softened.
2. Add the mushrooms and cook for 3 minutes, until the mushrooms have softened.
3. Add the vegetable broth, carrots, potatoes, celery, tomatoes and beans. Bring to a boil and reduce heat to a simmer. Simmer for 20 minutes.
4. Add the oregano, thyme and red pepper flakes. Simmer for 5 more minutes.
5. Remove from heat and stir in the parsley and basil. Season with salt and black pepper, to taste.

Nutrition Information:
Per serving: Calories: 210 kcal, Carbs: 37 g, Protein: 9 g, Fat: 3.2 g, Fiber: 8 g, Sugar: 6 g

18. Tomato and Parsley Minestrone Soup

This hearty Tomato and Parsley Minestrone Soup is the perfect combination of flavors and textures. The fresh parsley and tomatoes provide brightness and flavor to the soup, while the beans and vegetable stock add depth and body. You'll love this easy and healthy soup!

Serving: 4-6 | Preparation Time: 10 minutes | Ready Time: 25 minutes

Ingredients:
- 2 tablespoons olive oil
- 1 onion, diced
- 2 carrots, diced
- 2 celery stalks, diced
- 3 cloves garlic, minced
- 1 teaspoon dried oregano
- 2 (15 ounce) cans diced tomatoes
- 6 cups vegetable broth
- 1/2 cup dried lentils
- 2 (15 ounce) cans white beans, drained
- 1/2 cup fresh parsley, chopped
- Salt and pepper, to taste

Instructions:
1. Heat the olive oil in a large pot over medium heat. Add the onion, carrots, celery and garlic and cook for about 5 minutes, until vegetables are softened.
2. Add the oregano, diced tomatoes, vegetable broth, lentils and white beans. Bring to a boil then reduce the heat and simmer for 15 minutes, stirring occasionally.
3. Stir in the parsley, salt and pepper. Simmer for 5 more minutes.
4. Serve warm with crusty bread.

Nutrition Information:
Calories: 246 calories per serving, Fat: 4.4 grams, Carbohydrates: 42.5 grams, Protein: 11.2 grams

19. Butternut Squash Minestrone Soup

Butternut Squash Minestrone Soup is a deliciously flavorful and comforting soup. It is one of the most nutritious paleo soups out there as it is full of vegetables and healthy ingredients.

Serving: 4-6 | Preparation Time: 5 minutes | Ready Time: 40 minutes

Ingredients:

- 2 tablespoons of extra virgin olive oil
- 1 onion, diced
- 4 cloves of garlic, minced
- 1 teaspoon of dried oregano
- 2 cups of diced butternut squash
- 2 chopped celery stalks
- 1 diced carrot
- 1 can of diced tomatoes
- 2 tablespoons of tomato paste
- 4 cups of vegetable broth
- 1 can of cannellini beans, drained and rinsed
- 2 tablespoons of freshly chopped parsley
- Salt and pepper, to taste

Instructions:
1. Heat the oil in a large pot over medium heat and add the onion, garlic, and oregano. Cook until the onions are softened, about 2 minutes.
2. Add the butternut squash, celery, and carrot. Cook until the vegetables are starting to soften, about 5 minutes.
3. Add the diced tomatoes, tomato paste, and vegetable broth. Bring the mixture to a boil then reduce to a simmer and cook for 10 minutes.
4. Add the beans and parsley and cook for another 10 minutes.
5. Season with salt and pepper, to taste.

Nutrition Information:
Calories: 190 kcal, Carbohydrates: 28 g, Protein: 6 g, Fat: 7 g, Saturated Fat: 1 g, Sodium: 488 mg, Potassium: 593 mg, Fiber: 6 g, Sugar: 6 g, Vitamin A: 9312 IU, Vitamin C: 62 mg, Calcium: 138 mg, Iron: 4 mg

20. Coconut Curry Minestrone Soup

Coconut Curry Minestrone Soup is a creamy, sweet and savory soup that is packed with flavorful Asian spices and subtle coconut notes. Comforting, nourishing and delicious, it's a soup that's sure to be enjoyed by all.

Serving: 4 | Preparation Time: 10 minutes | Ready Time: 45 minutes

Ingredients:
- 1 tablespoon extra-virgin olive oil
- 1 onion, diced
- 2-3 cloves garlic, minced
- 1 red bell pepper, diced
- 1 teaspoon ground turmeric
- 2 tablespoons red curry paste
- 1 can (14.5 ounces) diced tomatoes
- 1 can (15 ounces) chickpeas, drained and rinsed
- 6 cups vegetable broth
- 1 can (14.5 ounces) coconut milk
- 2 potatoes, diced
- 2 carrots, diced
- 1 cup green beans
- 1 teaspoon sea salt

Instructions:
1. Heat the olive oil in a large pot over medium heat and add the onion, garlic, and bell pepper. Cook for about 5 minutes until soft.
2. Add the turmeric and curry paste, stirring for about 1 minute.
3. Add the diced tomatoes, chickpeas, vegetable broth, coconut milk, potatoes, carrots, and green beans. Stir and bring to a boil.
4. Reduce heat to low, cover and simmer for 30 minutes, or until the vegetables are tender.
5. Taste the broth and season with salt and more curry paste, if desired.

Nutrition Information:
Serving Size: 1/4 of total recipe, Calories: 280, Fat: 16g, Carbohydrates: 31g, Protein: 9g, Sodium: 706mg, Fiber: 7g

21. Corn and Bacon Minestrone Soup

Corn and Bacon Minestrone Soup is a hearty, Italian-style soup made with sweet corn, crunchy bacon, and a medley of vegetables cooked in flavorful, tomato-based broth.

Serving: 6 | Preparation Time: 15 minutes | Ready Time: 45 minutes

Ingredients:
-6-8 slices of bacon, diced
- 1 large onion, diced
- 1 celery stalk, chopped
- 1 large carrot, sliced
- 2 cloves garlic, minced
- 2 tablespoons olive oil
- 2 tablespoons tomato paste
- 6 cups chicken broth
- 2 cups sweet corn
- 1/2 cup macaroni
- 2 cups diced kale or spinach
- Salt and pepper, to taste
- 1 teaspoon Italian seasoning
- Fresh parsley for garnish, optional

Instructions:
1. In a large pot, cook bacon over medium heat until crisp, about 8 minutes.
2. Discard all but 1 tablespoon of the bacon grease and add the onion, celery, carrot, garlic, and a pinch of salt and pepper, to the pot. Cook until all vegetables are tender, about 5-7 minutes.
3. Add tomato paste and olive oil and stir to combine. Cook for 1-2 minutes more.
4. Add chicken broth, corn, macaroni, Italian seasoning, and a pinch of salt and pepper. Simmer until macaroni is tender, about 20-25 minutes.
5. Add kale or spinach and cook until wilted, about 2-3 minutes.
6. Taste for seasoning and adjust if necessary.
7. Serve with fresh parsley and extra bacon on top, if desired.

Nutrition Information:
Calories: 185; Fat: 9.5g; Carbohydrate: 22.5g; Protein: 6.5g; Sodium: 955 mg; Sugar: 5.5g

22. Bacon and Pasta Minestrone Soup

Bacon and Pasta Minestrone Soup is a hearty and flavorful dish perfect for cold winter days. Featuring pancetta, vegetables, and Parmesan cheese, this dish is sure to please with its bold taste and inviting aroma. Serving 8-10 people, this soup can be prepared in 30 minutes and ready in 45, making it a simple and delicious weeknight meal.

Serving: 8-10 people | Preparation Time: 30 minutes | Ready Time: 45 minutes

Ingredients:
- 8-10 slices of pancetta
- 2 tablespoons butter
- 2 carrots, diced
- 1 onion, diced
- 2 celery stalks, diced
- 2 cloves garlic, minced
- 5-6 cups vegetable or chicken broth
- 1 cup small pasta shells
- 2 cups diced potatoes
- 2 cups corn kernels
- 2 cans cannellini beans, drained and rinsed
- 2 tablespoons tomato paste
- 1/2 teaspoon dried oregano
- 1 teaspoon fresh parsley, chopped
- 1/4 teaspoon freshly ground black pepper
- 1/4 cup freshly grated Parmesan cheese

Instructions:
1. Heat a large dutch oven or soup pot over medium heat and cook the pancetta until crispy. Remove to a plate lined with a paper towel.
2. Melt the butter in the pot and add the carrots, onion, celery, and garlic. Cook for about 5 minutes until the vegetables are softened.
3. Add the broth, pasta shells, potatoes, corn, beans, tomato paste, oregano, and pepper. Increase the heat to bring the soup to a boil.
4. Reduce the heat to low and simmer for about 25 minutes, stirring occasionally, until the pasta and potatoes are tender.
5. Add the parsley and Parmesan cheese and stir to combine.
6. Serve with the crispy pancetta and additional Parmesan, if desired.

Nutrition Information:
Calories: 251, Total fat: 7g, Saturated fat: 3g, Cholesterol: 13mg, Sodium: 785mg, Carbohydrates: 38g, Fiber: 6g, Protein: 10g

23. Potato and Celery Minestrone Soup

Potato and Celery Minestrone Soup is a flavorful and easy-to-make soup that can be enjoyed all year round. This hearty and filling soup is sure to become a family favorite!

Serving: 4 | Preparation Time: 15 minutes | Ready Time: 40 minutes

Ingredients:
- 2 tablespoons olive oil
- 1 onion, chopped
- 2 cloves garlic, minced
- 2 carrots, diced
- 2 celery stalks, diced
- 4 potatoes, peeled and diced
- 2 quarts vegetable broth
- 2 cups diced tomatoes
- 2 bay leaves
- 1 tablespoon fresh parsley, chopped
- 1 teaspoon dried oregano
- 1 teaspoon dried basil
- Salt and freshly ground black pepper to taste

Instructions:
1. Heat the olive oil in a large pot over medium heat. Add the onion, garlic, carrots and celery and sauté for 5 minutes.
2. Add the potatoes, vegetable broth, tomatoes, bay leaves, parsley, oregano and basil. Cover and bring to a boil, then reduce the heat to low and simmer for 30 minutes.
3. Season with salt and pepper to taste and simmer for an additional 5 minutes.
4. Remove the bay leaves and serve.

Nutrition Information:
Per serving: Calories: 111, Total Fat: 6g, Cholesterol: 0mg, Sodium: 831mg, Carbohydrates: 13g, Fiber: 4g, Protein: 3g

24. Broccoli and Orzo Minestrone Soup

This Broccoli and Orzo Minestrone Soup is a cozy, comforting, and delicious way to enjoy seasonal veggies! It's packed with vitamins and minerals and can be ready in under 45 minutes.

Serving: 6 | Preparation Time: 20 minutes

Ingredients:
- 2 tablespoons olive oil
- 1 large onion, diced
- 1 large carrot, diced
- 2 cloves garlic, chopped
- 4 cups vegetable broth
- 1/2 cup orzo
- 1 1/2 cups broccoli florets
- 1/4 teaspoon freshly ground black pepper
- 1/4 teaspoon dried oregano
- 1/4 teaspoon hot red pepper flakes

Instructions:
1. Heat the olive oil in a large pot over medium heat. Add the onion, carrot, and garlic and cook, stirring occasionally, until the onion is softened and lightly browned, about 3 minutes.
2. Add the vegetable broth, orzo, broccoli, black pepper, oregano, and red pepper flakes. Bring the mixture to a boil, then reduce the heat to low, cover the pot, and let simmer for 20 minutes.
3. Taste for seasonings, and adjust if desired. Serve hot.

Nutrition Information:
Calories: 148, Fat: 5 g, Carbohydrates: 20 g, Protein: 5 g

25. White Bean and Arugula Minestrone Soup

This delicious White Bean and Arugula Minestrone Soup is packed with vegetables and beans and it has a flavorful and comforting broth. It's perfect for a cold day, or something special for family or guests.

SERVING: 4 servings | Preparation Time: 15 minutes | Ready Time: 45 minutes

INGREDIENTS:
- 2 tablespoons olive oil
- 1/2 onion, chopped
- 4 garlic cloves, minced
- 2 carrots, chopped
- 4 cups vegetable broth
- 2 tomatoes, chopped
- 1 teaspoon dried oregano
- 2 cups cooked white beans
- 2 cups baby spinach
- 2 cups arugula
- 2 tablespoons freshly grated Parmesan cheese
- Sea salt, to taste

INSTRUCTION:
1. Heat olive oil in a pot over medium heat. Add onions and garlic and sauté for 2-3 minutes.
2. Add carrots and broth, bring to a boil and reduce heat to low. Simmer for 15 minutes.
3. Add tomatoes, oregano and white beans and simmer for an additional 10 minutes.
4. Add spinach and arugula and simmer for another 5 minutes.
5. Turn off heat and stir in Parmesan cheese and season with salt. Serve warm.

NUTRITION INFORMATION:
Serving Size: 1 bowl, Calories: 281, Fat: 9g, Carbohydrates: 37g, Protein: 13g, Fiber: 13g

26. Cannellini Bean and Tomato Minestrone Soup

This Cannellini Bean and Tomato Minestrone Soup is the perfect combination of vegetables, beans, and light tomato broth. All the ingredients combine to create a super comforting and flavorful dish that is sure to please.

Serving: Serves 6-8 people | Preparation Time: 10 minutes | Ready Time: 40 minutes

Ingredients:
- 2 tablespoons olive oil
- 1 large onion, chopped
- 3 cloves garlic, minced
- 1 sprig fresh rosemary
- 2 cups diced carrots
- 2 cups diced celery
- 4 cups vegetable broth
- 2 (14-ounce) cans diced tomatoes
- 2 (14-ounce) cans cannellini beans, rinsed and drained
- 2 cups small pasta, such as elbow macaroni
- 2 tablespoons chopped fresh parsley
- Salt and pepper, to taste

Instructions:
1. Heat olive oil in a large pot over medium heat. Add the onion and garlic, and cook for 2-3 minutes until lightly browned.
2. Add the rosemary, carrots, and celery, and stir to combine. Cook for 4-5 more minutes until the vegetables are softened.
3. Pour in the vegetable broth, tomatoes, cannellini beans, pasta, and parsley, and stir to combine.
4. Bring the mixture to a simmer and cook for 20-25 minutes, stirring occasionally, until the pasta is cooked through.
5. Taste the soup and season with salt and pepper, to taste. Serve warm.

Nutrition Information:
Per 1 serving: 237 Cals | 20g Fat | 16g Carbs | 3g Protein

27. Orzo and Pesto Minestrone Soup

Orzo and Pesto Minestrone Soup is a light and flavorful soup that is perfect for the start of a meal. This soup combines the heartiness of a vegetable-filled minestrone, with the bright flavor of pesto and the slight chewiness of orzo pasta for a simple yet tasty dish.

Serving: 4-6 | Preparation Time: 10 minutes | Ready Time: 35 minutes

Ingredients:
- 1 Tbsp olive oil
- 2 cloves of garlic, minced
- 1 onion, chopped
- 4 cups vegetable broth
- 1 can (14.5 oz) diced tomatoes
- 1 can (15.5 oz) small white beans, drained
- 1/2 cup orzo pasta
- 2 cups of fresh spinach
- 2-3 Tbsp of pesto

Instructions:
1. In a large pot, heat the olive oil over medium heat and add the garlic and onion. Cook until the onions are transparent, stirring often.
2. Add the vegetable broth, diced tomatoes, and small white beans and bring to a boil.
3. Reduce heat to low and stir in the orzo pasta. Cook for 10 minutes.
4. Add the spinach and pesto to the soup and stir to combine. Cook for an additional 5 minutes.
5. Serve the soup with crusty bread to soak up all of the delicious flavors.

Nutrition Information:
Calories: 183, Fat: 8.6g, Cholesterol: 0mg, Sodium: 475mg, Carbohydrates: 24.6g, Protein: 6.4g, Fiber: 5.3g.

28. Gnocchi and Spinach Minestrone Soup

Gnocchi and Spinach Minestrone Soup – a delicious, hearty soup perfect for any time of the year. This dish is packed full of flavor, nutrient-rich vegetables and protein, making it a great meal for vegetarians and omnivores alike.

Serving: 4-6 | Preparation Time: 10 minutes | Ready Time: 25 minutes

Ingredients:
- 1 tablespoon extra-virgin olive oil
- 1 onion, diced
- 2 garlic cloves, minced
- 1 teaspoon dried oregano
- 4 cups vegetable broth
- 2 cans (14.5 ounces each) diced tomatoes, with juices
- 1 cup uncooked Gnocchi
- 2 cups fresh spinach, chopped
- 2 tablespoons chopped fresh parsley
- 1/2 teaspoon salt
- 1/4 teaspoon freshly ground black pepper

Instructions:
1. Heat oil in a large soup pot over medium heat. Add onion, garlic and oregano, and cook, stirring occasionally, until onions are softened and lightly browned, about 5 minutes.
2. Add broth, tomatoes with juices, gnocchi and bring to a boil. Reduce heat to medium-low and simmer for 15 minutes.
3. Add spinach and simmer for five more minutes.
4. Ladle into individual bowls and top with parsley and a sprinkle of black pepper.

Nutrition Information:
Serving Size: 1/4 of Recipe • Calories: 134 • Carbohydrates: 22.6g • Protein: 5.3g • Fat: 3.3g • Saturated Fat: 0.5g • Cholesterol: 0mg • Sodium: 707mg • Fiber: 3.2g • Sugar: 5.3g

29. Rice and Sausage Minestrone Soup

This delicious Rice and Sausage Minestrone Soup is a great way to make a comforting meal for your family. It is filled with the goodness of fresh vegetables, nutritious rice and hearty sausage that create a flavorful combination.

Serving: 8 | Preparation Time: 10 minutes | Ready Time: 45 minutes

Ingredients:
- 1 tablespoons olive oil
- 2 cloves garlic, minced
- 1/2 onion, chopped
- 1/2 cup chopped celery
- 1/2 cup diced carrots
- 4 cups chicken broth
- 1 cup uncooked dry brown or white rice
- 1 (14.5-ounce) can diced tomatoes
- 1 teaspoon dried oregano
- 1/2 teaspoon dried basil
- 1/2 teaspoon salt
- 2 (14.5-ounce) cans cannellini beans, rinsed and drained
- 1 (14-ounce) link Italian sausage, cooked and sliced

Instruction:
1. In a large pot over medium heat, heat oil. Add garlic, onion, celery, and carrots; cook and stir for 3 minutes.
2. Add broth, rice, tomatoes, oregano, basil and salt; bring to a boil.
3. Reduce heat to medium-low and simmer for 20 minutes, stirring occasionally.
4. Add beans and sausage; cook for an additional 10 minutes or until rice is cooked through.

Nutrition Information:
Per serving, 176 calories, 7.5 g fat, 24.5 g carbohydrates, 7.5 g protein

30. Farro and Swiss Chard Minestrone Soup

Farro and Swiss Chard Minestrone Soup is an Italian classic that's a hearty and flavorful way to get your vegetables in. With farro providing a chewy texture, Swiss chard providing a floral flavor, and vegetables offering an array of colors and nutrients, this soup will be a favorite in no time.

Serving: 6-8 | Preparation Time: 15 Minutes | Ready Time: 40 minutes

Ingredients:

- 1 tablespoon olive oil
- 1 onion, diced
- 2 garlic cloves, minced
- 2 carrots, diced
- 2 ribs celery, diced
- 4 cups vegetable broth
- 2 cups Swiss chard, chopped
- 1 cup farro
- 2 cups diced tomatoes
- 2 tablespoons tomato paste
- 1 teaspoon dried oregano
- 1 teaspoon dried basil
- 1 teaspoon kosher salt
- 1/4 teaspoon freshly ground black pepper
- 2 (15-ounce) cans cannellini beans, drained and rinsed

Instructions:

1. Heat olive oil in a large pot over medium-high heat.
2. Add onion, garlic, carrots, and celery and cook, stirring occasionally, for 4 minutes.
3. Add broth, chard, farro, tomatoes, tomato paste, oregano, basil, salt, and pepper.
4. Bring to a boil, reduce heat to medium-low, and simmer for 25 minutes.
5. Add beans and simmer for an additional 10 minutes.
6. Serve warm.

Nutrition Information:

Serving size: 1 cup (7oz/198g), Amount Per Serving: Calories 297, Total Fat 7g (10% DV), Sodium 703mg (30% DV), Total Carbohydrates 46g (16% DV), Dietary Fiber 11g (42% DV), Total Sugars 4g, Protein 13g, Vitamin A (37% DV), Vitamin C (37% DV), Calcium (18% DV), Iron (30% DV).

31. Red Lentil Minestrone Soup

Red Lentil Minestrone Soup is a hearty, vegetarian soup perfect for a chilly evening. It has a mix of earthy red lentils, tender vegetables, and succulent broth that come together to create a delicious meal.

Serving: 6-8 | Preparation Time: 15 minutes | Ready Time: 40 minutes

Ingredients:
- 1/4 cup extra-virgin olive oil
- 1 small onion, diced
- 2 cloves garlic, minced
- 2 stalks celery, chopped
- 2 carrots, chopped
- 2 small zucchini, chopped
- 2 teaspoon Italian seasoning blend
- 1 cup red lentils
- 6 cups vegetable broth
- 1 can (14 oz) diced tomatoes
- 1/2 teaspoon sea salt
- 1/4 teaspoon freshly ground black pepper

Instructions:
1. Heat oil in a large pot over medium heat.
2. Add in onion, garlic, celery, carrots and zucchini. Cook for about 5 minutes, stirring occasionally.
3. Stir in Italian seasoning, lentils and vegetable broth.
4. Bring to a boil then reduce heat to low and simmer for 25 minutes.
5. Stir in diced tomatoes and season with sea salt and pepper.
6. Cook for an additional 10 minutes.

Nutrition Information (Per Serving):

Calories: 156, Fat: 7g, Carbohydrates: 19.7g, Protein: 6g, Sodium: 923mg, Fiber: 7.7g

32. Italian-Style Bean Minestrone Soup

Modeled after the classic Italian dish, this Italian-Style Bean Minestrone Soup is a hearty and healthy one-pot meal perfect for chilly fall and winter days.

Serving: 6-8 | Preparation Time: 15 minutes

Ingredients:
- 1 large onion chopped
- 1/2 teaspoon garlic powder
- 2 tablespoons of olive oil
- 1 red pepper; diced
- 2 cloves garlic; minced
- 2 cups diced tomatoes
- 2 cups vegetable broth
- 4 cups cooked white beans of your choice; drained and rinsed
- 1/2 cup of orzo pasta
- 2 tablespoons Italian seasoning
- Salt and pepper to taste
- Freshly chopped parsley for serving

Instructions
1. In a large pot, heat the olive oil over a medium-high flame and add the onions, peppers, and garlic. Cook for 3 minutes, stirring occasionally to prevent burning.
2. Add the tomatoes, vegetable broth, beans, orzo, Italian seasoning, salt, and pepper and stir until combined. Bring the soup to a boil, reduce to a low simmer, and cook for 10 minutes, stirring occasionally.
3. When the orzo is fully cooked, serve the soup hot with a sprinkle of freshly chopped parsley.

Nutrition Information:
Calories: 260 per serving, Fat: 4.7g, Carbohydrates: 36.8g, Protein: 11.1g

33. Butternut Squash and Sausage Minestrone Soup

Butternut Squash and Sausage Minestrone Soup: Get your taste buds ready for this delicious and comforting soup! This hearty and flavorful soup is made with butternut squash, Italian sausage and veggies, making it a unique and delicious twist on traditional minestrone soup.

Servings: 8 | Preparation Time: 10 minutes | Ready Time: 45 minutes

Ingredients:
- 1 tablespoon olive oil
- 1 small onion, diced
- 1 red bell pepper, diced
- 3 cloves garlic, minced
- 1 pound Italian sausage, ground
- 3 tablespoons tomato paste
- 3 stalks celery, diced
- 6 cups vegetable stock
- 2 14-ounce cans cannelini beans, drained and rinsed
- 1 butternut squash, peeled and cut into small cubes
- 2 teaspoons Italian seasoning
- Salt and black pepper, to taste
- 1/4 teaspoon red pepper flakes
- 1 cup small pasta (such as ditalini or elbow), uncooked

Instructions:
1. Heat olive oil in a large pot or Dutch oven over medium heat. Add in the onion and bell pepper and season with salt and pepper. Cook until the vegetables are beginning to soften, about 5 minutes.
2. Add in the garlic and cook for an additional minute.
3. Add in the sausage and cook, breaking it up into small pieces, until it is no longer pink, about 5 minutes.
4. Add in the tomato paste, celery, vegetable stock, beans, butternut squash, and Italian seasoning and stir to combine.

5. Bring to a boil, then cover, reduce heat and simmer for 30 minutes.
6. Add in the pasta and continue to cook until the pasta is just al dente, about 10-15 minutes.
7. Add additional salt and pepper, to taste.

Nutrition Information:
Each serving contains approximately 180 calories, 8g fat, 17g carbohydrate, 11g protein.

34. Quinoa and Kale Minestrone Soup

This Quinoa and Kale Minestrone Soup is an incredibly hearty and comforting vegetarian meal that's full of fresh vegetables, quinoa and great flavor. Perfect for a chilly night, this vegan soup is easy to prepare, but is sure to impress.

Serving: Serves 8 | Preparation Time: 15 minutes | Ready Time: 40 minutes

Ingredients:
- 2 tablespoons olive oil
- 1 yellow onion, diced
- 2 carrots, peeled and diced
- 3 celery stalks, diced
- 4 cloves garlic, minced
- 1 teaspoon dried oregano
- 1 bay leaf
- 1 teaspoon kosher salt
- 1 teaspoon black pepper
- 6 cups vegetable broth
- 2 cups cooked quinoa
- 2 (15-ounce) cans diced tomatoes
- 1 (15-ounce) can cannellini beans, drained and rinsed
- 1 (5-ounce) bag chopped kale
- 2 tablespoons balsamic vinegar

Instructions:

1. Heat the olive oil in a large pot or Dutch oven over medium heat. Add the onion, carrots and celery and sauté for 7 minutes.
2. Add the garlic, oregano, bay leaf, salt and pepper, and saute for 1 minute until fragrant.
3. Add the vegetable broth, quinoa, tomatoes, beans and kale, and bring to a simmer. Simmer for 20 minutes.
4. Remove the bay leaf, and stir in the balsamic vinegar.

Nutrition Information:
Per Serving (1 cup): Calories: 192, Total Fat: 4.7 g, Saturated Fat: 0.7 g, Sodium: 566 mg, Total Carbohydrates: 28.7 g, Dietary Fiber: 6.0 g, Sugars: 6.3 g, Protein: 8.2 g.

35. Mexican-Style Minestrone Soup

Spicy, robust, and full of flavor, this Mexican-Style Minestrone Soup is a fantastic way to add some zest to your meal! With plenty of vegetables, kidney beans, and salsa, this delicious soup is perfect for lunch or dinner.

Serving: 8 | Preparation Time: 15 minutes | Ready Time: 30 minutes

Ingredients:
- 2 tablespoons olive oil
- 1 yellow onion, chopped
- 1 red bell pepper, chopped
- 1 teaspoon chili powder
- 1 teaspoon cumin
- 2 cloves garlic, minced
- 4 cups vegetable broth
- 1 (14.5-ounce) can diced tomatoes
- 1 (15-ounce) can kidney beans, drained and rinsed
- 1 (4.5-ounce) can chopped green chiles
- 2 cups frozen corn
- 2 cups cooked black beans
- 2 tablespoons salsa
- 2 cups cooked macaroni
- 1/4 cup chopped fresh cilantro

Instructions:
1. Heat the oil in a large pot over medium-high heat. Add the onion, bell pepper, chili powder, and cumin and cook, stirring, until the vegetables are softened, about 4 minutes. Add the garlic and cook for 1 minute more.
2. Add the vegetable broth, diced tomatoes, kidney beans, green chiles, corn, black beans, salsa, macaroni and cilantro. Bring to a boil, reduce the heat and simmer until the vegetables are tender, about 20 minutes.
3. Serve hot. Enjoy!

Nutrition Information (per serving):
Calories: 320, Total Fat: 7 g, Saturated Fat: 1 g, Cholesterol: 0 mg, Sodium: 590 mg, Carbohydrate: 53 g, Dietary Fiber: 8 g, Protein: 10 g

36. Baked Bean Minestrone Soup

Try this cozy, yet flavorful and nourishing one-pot soup for your next family meal. Baked bean minestrone soup is a delicious and hearty soup, infused with garlic and herbs, and great for vegetarians, vegans, and meat-eaters alike.

Serving: Makes 6-8 servings | Preparation Time: 20 minutes | Ready Time: 40 minutes

Ingredients:
-2 tablespoons olive oil
-1 large onion, diced
-3 cloves garlic, minced
-3 stalks celery, diced
-3 carrots, diced
-1 (14.5-ounce) can diced tomatoes in juice
-2 teaspoons dried basil
-1 teaspoon dried oregano
-1 teaspoon dried thyme
-1/2 teaspoon dried rosemary
-1/2 teaspoon freshly ground black pepper
-1 bay leaf
-4 cups vegetable broth or stock

-3 (15-ounce) cans navy beans, rinsed and drained
-1 (15-ounce) can cannellini beans, rinsed and drained
-2 cups chopped kale
-2 tablespoons freshly chopped Italian parsley, for garnish

Instructions:
1. Heat the olive oil in a large pot over medium heat. Add the onion and sauté for 4 minutes.
2. Add the garlic, celery, and carrots, and cook for 5 more minutes, stirring occasionally.
3. Add the diced tomatoes, basil, oregano, thyme, rosemary, black pepper, and bay leaf and cook for 3 minutes, stirring occasionally.
4. Add the vegetable broth and both cans of beans. Bring to a boil, then reduce heat to low and simmer for 15 minutes.
5. Add the kale and simmer for 10 more minutes.
6. Ladle into soup bowls and garnish with fresh parsley.

Nutrition Information:
Per Serving: Calories: 291, Total fat: 5 grams, Saturated fat: 1 gram, Cholesterol: 0 milligrams, Sodium: 892 milligrams, Total carbohydrates: 49 grams, Dietary fiber: 14 grams, Protein: 16 grams

37. Cannellini Bean and Mushroom Minestrone Soup

Cannellini Bean and Mushroom Minestrone Soup is a hearty vegetarian soup that is nutrition packed and loaded with flavor. Filled with tender cannellini beans, juicy mushrooms, flavorful vegetables, and a touch of heat, this soup is your new go-to for a quick and healthy meal.

Serving: 4-6 | Preparation Time: 20 minutes | Ready Time: 30 minutes

Ingredients:
- 2 tablespoons olive oil
- 1 medium onion, chopped
- 3 cloves garlic, minced
- 4 cups vegetable broth
- 2 cans cannellini beans, drained and rinsed

- 2 cups diced mushrooms
- 1 carrot, finely chopped
- 1 celery stalk, finely chopped
- 1 cup diced zucchini
- 1 teaspoon dried oregano
- 1/2 teaspoon red pepper flakes
- 1/2 teaspoon black pepper
- 2 tablespoons freshly chopped parsley
- 2 tablespoons freshly chopped basil
- Grated Parmesan cheese, to garnish

Instructions:
1. Heat the olive oil in a large pot over medium heat.
2. Once the oil is hot, add the onion and garlic and cook for about 5 minutes, stirring often.
3. Add the vegetable broth, beans, mushrooms, carrots, celery, zucchini, oregano, red pepper flakes, and black pepper.
4. Bring the soup to a boil and then reduce the heat to low and simmer for about 15 minutes, or until the vegetables are tender.
5. Add the parsley and basil and stir to combine.
6. Serve hot with a sprinkle of Parmesan cheese, if desired.

Nutrition Information:
Per serving: Calories: 200, Fat: 8g, Saturated fat: 1g, Carbohydrates: 26g, Fiber: 8g, Protein: 9g, Sugar: 5g, Cholesterol: 0mg, Sodium: 500mg

38. Olive and Tomato Minestrone Soup

Olive and Tomato Minestrone Soup is a delicious, vibrant and healthy bowl of soup loaded with fresh vegetables, garlic, beans and pasta. Packed full of flavor, this light and healthy soup is sure to satisfy everyone around the table.

Serving Size: 4-6 people | Preparation Time: 10 minutes | Ready Time: 40 minutes.

Ingredients:
- 2 tablespoons olive oil

- 1 white onion, diced
- 2 cloves garlic, minced
- 2 carrots, peeled and diced
- 2 celery stalks, diced
- 1 red bell pepper, seeded and diced
- 2 teaspoons dried oregano
- 2 teaspoons dried basil
- 1 teaspoon dried thyme
- 2 tablespoons tomato paste
- 6 cups vegetable broth
- 1 (14.5 ounce) can diced tomatoes
- 1 (15 ounce) can red kidney beans, drained and rinsed
- 1 (15 ounce) can cannellini beans, drained and rinsed
- 1 cup uncooked macaroni or other small pasta
- 1 cup fresh spinach, roughly chopped
- Kosher salt and freshly ground black pepper, to taste

Instructions:
1. Heat olive oil in a large pot over medium heat. Add onion and garlic and cook, stirring frequently, until onions have become translucent, about 3-4 minutes.
2. Stir in carrots, celery, and bell pepper and cook, stirring occasionally, until vegetables have softened and lightly caramelized, about 6-7 minutes.
3. Add oregano, basil, and thyme and cook until fragrant, about 1 minute.
4. Stir in tomato paste and cook, stirring constantly, until lightly browned, 3-4 minutes.
5. Pour in vegetable broth, scraping up any browned bits from the bottom of the pot. Stir in diced tomatoes, red kidney beans, cannellini beans, and pasta.
6. Bring to a boil; reduce heat and simmer until pasta is cooked through, about 12-15 minutes.
7. Stir in spinach and let cook until wilted, about 2 minutes. Season with salt and pepper, to taste.

Nutrition Information:
Calories: 350 Fat: 7.5 grams, Protein: 12.5 grams, Carbohydrates: 56 grams, Fiber: 10 grams, Sugar: 6 grams, Sodium: 1093 milligrams

39. Chickpea and Spinach Minestrone Soup

Chickpea and Spinach Minestrone Soup is a hearty and healthy soup perfect for lunch or dinner. This delicious soup is full of vegetable goodness, with chickpeas and spinach providing protein, vitamins, and minerals. It's sure to satisfy everybody's taste buds and leave everyone wanting seconds!

Serving: 8 | Preparation Time: 10 minutes | Ready Time: 30 minutes

Ingredients:
- 2 tablespoons olive oil
- 2 cloves garlic, minced
- 1 onion, diced
- 2 celery stalks, diced
- 2 carrots, diced
- 2 cups vegetable broth
- 2 tablespoons tomato paste
- 4 cups cooked chickpeas
- 4 cups baby spinach
- 2 tablespoons fresh parsley, chopped
- 2 tablespoons fresh basil, chopped
- 1 teaspoon salt
- 1/2 teaspoon pepper

Instructions:
1. Heat the olive oil in a large pot over medium-high heat.
2. Add the garlic, onion, celery, and carrots and cook for about 5 minutes, stirring frequently.
3. Add the vegetable broth, tomato paste, chickpeas, and spinach and bring to a simmer.
4. Cook for about 10 minutes, stirring occasionally.
5. Add the parsley, basil, salt, and pepper and stir to combine.
6. Reduce the heat to low and simmer for an additional 10 minutes.
7. Serve warm with crusty bread.

Nutrition Information (per serving):
Calories: 296, Protein: 12.3g, Carbohydrates: 44.3g, Fat: 8.7g, Fiber: 9.2g, Sugars: 6.2g, Sodium: 665mg

40. Rice and Broccoli Minestrone Soup

Rice and Broccoli Minestrone Soup is a veggie-packed, comforting bowl of goodness! It's easy to make and uses simple ingredients. Serve it with crusty bread or a side salad for a filling and nutritious meal.

Serving: 4-6 | Preparation Time: 10 min | Ready Time: 40 min

Ingredients:
-1 tablespoons olive oil
-1 small onion, finely chopped
-2 garlic cloves, minced
-6 cups vegetable broth
-1 (14-oz) can diced tomatoes
-1 teaspoon Italian seasoning
-2 cups broccoli florets
-3/4 cup uncooked long grain white rice
-Salt and freshly ground black pepper to taste

Instructions:
1. Heat the olive oil in a large Dutch oven over medium heat. Add the onion and cook for about 5 minutes until softened. Add the garlic and cook for an additional 1 minute.
2. Add the broth, diced tomatoes, Italian seasoning, broccoli, and rice. Mix well and bring the soup to a boil. Reduce the heat to low, cover, and simmer for 30-35 minutes, stirring occasionally, until the rice is cooked.
3. Taste and adjust the seasoning if needed with salt and pepper.
4. Serve the soup warm.

Nutrition information (Serving Size – 1 cup):
Calories: 155, Protein: 4g, Fat: 4g, Carbohydrates: 26g, Fiber: 3g, Sugar: 5g, Sodium: 517 mg

41. Carrot and Potato Minestrone Soup

Try this hearty soup that takes advantage of carrots and potatoes for a stocked up pantry meal. Carrot and Potato Minestrone Soup is chock full of vegetables and beans and makes a great meatless meal.

Serving: 6-8 | Preparation Time: 10 minutes | Ready Time: 30 minutes

Ingredients:
-1/4 cup olive oil
-1/2 diced yellow onion
-3 large carrots, diced
-3 cloves garlic, minced
-3 celery stalks, diced
-2 lbs potatoes, peeled and diced
-1 teaspoon dried oregano
-1 teaspoon dried basil
-1 can kidney beans, drained and rinsed
-1 can diced tomatoes
-1 quart vegetable broth
-2 cups water
-1 teaspoon salt
-Ground black pepper

Instructions:
1. In a large pot, heat olive oil over medium heat.
2. Add in onion, carrots, garlic, and celery, and sauté until vegetables soften, about 5-7 minutes.
3. Add in potatoes, dried oregano, dried basil, kidney beans, diced tomatoes, vegetable broth, water, and salt.
4. Increase heat to high and bring to a boil.
5. Reduce heat to low and simmer for 15-20 minutes or until vegetables are tender.
6. Taste and season with salt and ground black pepper, as desired.
7. Serve the soup warm.

Nutrition Information:
Calories: 156, Total Fat: 6g, Cholesterol: 0mg, Sodium: 481mg, Total Carbohydrate: 24g, Dietary Fiber: 5g, Sugars: 1g, Protein: 5g.

42. Baked Potato and Kale Minestrone Soup

This simple and flavorful Baked Potato and Kale Minestrone Soup is sure to be a crowd-pleaser. With hearty potatoes, fresh kale, and a mix of herbs and spices, it is both comforting and nutritious.

Serving: 6-8 | Preparation Time: 15 minutes | Ready Time: 35 minutes

Ingredients:
- 3 tablespoons olive oil
- 2 cloves garlic, minced
- 1 large onion, chopped
- 4 large potatoes, chopped
- 1 teaspoon dried thyme
- 1 teaspoon dried basil
- 4 cups vegetable broth
- 4 cups kale, chopped
- 2 cans (14.5 oz each) diced tomatoes, with juices
- 1/4 teaspoon fine sea salt
- Freshly ground black pepper, to taste
- 2 tablespoons chopped fresh parsley

Instructions:
1. Heat oil in a large pot over medium-high heat. Add garlic and onion and cook for 2 minutes, stirring occasionally.
2. Add potatoes, thyme and basil, and stir to combine. Cook for 4-5 minutes, stirring occasionally, until potatoes start to soften.
3. Add broth, kale, tomatoes and juices, salt and pepper and stir to combine. Bring to a boil, then reduce heat to low, cover pot and cook for 20 minutes, stirring occasionally.
4. Remove from heat and stir in parsley. Serve warm.

Nutrition Information:
Calories: 217, Total Fat: 7 g, Saturated Fat: 1 g, Cholesterol: 0 mg, Sodium: 703 mg, Potassium: 853 mg, Total Carbohydrates: 33 g, Dietary Fiber: 6 g, Sugars: 6 g, Protein: 7 g.

43. Bacon and Vegetable Minestrone Soup

Delight your taste buds with the delicious Bacon and Vegetable Minestrone Soup. Hearty and flavorful, this soup has delicious chunks of bacon and vegetables that make it the perfect meal for a cold winter day!

Serving: 6-8 | Preparation Time: 20 minutes | Ready Time: 40 minutes

Ingredients:
- 1 tablespoon olive oil
- 1 onion, diced
- 2 cloves garlic, minced
- 1 zucchini, diced
- 1 bell pepper, diced
- 3 stalks celery, diced
- 4 carrots, diced
- 1 red potato, diced
- 1/2 pound bacon, diced
- 6 cups vegetable broth
- 2 15-ounce cans diced tomatoes
- 2 15-ounce cans kidney beans, drained and rinsed
- 1/2 teaspoon dried thyme
- 2 tablespoons fresh parsley, chopped
- Salt and pepper, to taste

Instructions:
1. In a large pot, heat the olive oil over medium-high heat.
2. Add the onion, garlic, zucchini, bell pepper, celery, carrots and potato. Cook until the vegetables are softened, about 8 minutes.
3. Add the bacon and cook until the bacon is crisped, about 5 minutes.
4. Add the vegetable broth, diced tomatoes, kidney beans, thyme and parsley. Bring to a boil then reduce the heat to low and simmer for 20 minutes.
5. Taste and adjust seasoning with salt and pepper.

Nutrition Information:
Calories: 202, Fat: 7g, Carbohydrates: 28g, Protein: 7g, Fiber: 9g

44. Spanish-Style Minestrone Soup

Spanish-Style Minestrone Soup is an exceptionally flavorful, hearty soup loaded with vegetables, beans, spicy smoked paprika, and a hint of fresh tomatoes. This delicious and satisfying soup is perfect for a light lunch or dinner.

Serving: 6-8 | Preparation Time: 15 minutes | Ready Time: 40 minutes

Ingredients:
- 2 tablespoons olive oil
- 1 large onion, diced
- 1 red bell pepper, seeded and diced
- 4 cloves garlic, minced
- 2 teaspoons smoked paprika
- 2 cups vegetable stock
- 2 cups diced tomatoes
- 2 cups cooked cannellini beans
- 2 cups diced zucchini
- 2 cups thinly sliced kale
- 2 tablespoons chopped fresh parsley
- 2 bay leaves
- Salt and ground black pepper, to taste

Instructions:
1. Heat the olive oil in a large pot over medium heat.
2. Add the onion, bell pepper, and garlic and cook, stirring occasionally, until the vegetables begin to soften, about 5 minutes.
3. Add the smoked paprika and cook for another minute.
4. Add the vegetable stock, diced tomatoes, cannellini beans, zucchini, kale, parsley, and bay leaves and stir to combine. Bring to a boil, reduce the heat to medium-low, and simmer for 30 minutes.
5. Discard the bay leaves and season with salt and pepper.
6. Serve the soup warm.

Nutrition Information:
Calories: 267; Total Fat: 8.3 g; Sodium: 481 mg; Total Carbohydrates: 36.9 g; Protein: 12.1 g

45. White Bean and Bacon Minestrone Soup

White Bean and Bacon Minestrone Soup is a hearty and flavorful soup that combines the savory flavors of cured bacon and white beans with a variety of vegetables to create a comforting and delicious meal.

Serving: 4-6 | Preparation Time: 15 minutes | Ready Time: 45 minutes

Ingredients:
- 8 slices of bacon, diced
- 1 medium onion, diced
- 2 cloves garlic, minced
- 3 carrots, diced
- 3 celery stalks, diced
- 2 zucchini, diced
- 2 1/2 cups chicken broth
- 1 (28 ounce) can of diced tomatoes
- 1 (15 ounce) can of white beans, drained and rinsed
- 1 tsp of Italian seasoning
- Salt and pepper, to taste
- 1/4 cup of fresh parsley, chopped

Instructions:
1. In a large pot over medium heat, cook diced bacon until crisp.
2. Add in onion, garlic, carrots, and celery and cook for about 5 minutes.
3. Add in chicken broth, tomatoes, white beans, Italian seasoning, Salt and pepper. Bring to a boil, then reduce heat and simmer for 30 minutes.
4. Add in zucchini and continue to simmer for 10 minutes, or until vegetables are tender.
5. Garnish with fresh parsley and serve.

Nutrition Information:
Each serving contains approximately 200 calories, 9g fat, 19g carbohydrates, and 7g of protein.

46. Lentil and Zucchini Minestrone Soup

Lentil and Zucchini Minestrone Soup is a comforting and delicious combination of vegetables, beans and pasta in a hearty tomato broth.

Serving: 6-8 | Preparation Time: 15 minutes | Ready Time: 30 minutes

Ingredients:
- 2 tablespoons olive oil
- 1 onion, diced
- 2 carrots, diced
- 2 celery stalks, diced
- 4 garlic cloves, minced
- 1 teaspoon Italian seasoning
- 2 cups green lentils, rinsed
- 6 cups vegetable broth
- 28 ounce can crushed tomatoes
- 2 zucchini, diced
- 2 teaspoons salt
- 1/4 teaspoon ground black pepper
- 1/2 cup small pasta such as ditalini
- 1/4 cup chopped fresh parsley

Instructions:
1. Heat the oil in a large soup pot over medium heat. Add the onion, carrots, celery, garlic and Italian seasoning and sauté for 5 minutes, stirring occasionally, until the vegetables have softened.
2. Add the lentils and vegetable broth to the pot and stir to combine. Increase the heat to high and bring to a boil.
3. Once boiling, reduce heat to low, cover and simmer for 15 minutes.
4. Add the crushed tomatoes, zucchini, salt and pepper to the pot and stir to combine. Increase the heat to high and bring to a boil.
5. Once boiling, reduce heat to low, add the pasta and cover. Simmer for an additional 10 minutes, or until the pasta is tender.
6. Remove from heat and stir in the parsley. Serve warm.

Nutrition Information:
Serving size: 1 bowl, Calories: 233, Total Fat: 4g , Saturated Fat: 1g, Trans Fat: 0g, Cholesterol: 0mg , Sodium: 1199mg Total Carbohydrates: 38g, Dietary Fiber: 10g, Sugars: 6g, Protein: 10g

47. Quinoa and Edamame Minestrone Soup

Quinoa and Edamame Minestrone Soup is an extremely nourishing and complete meal in a bowl. The flavors of the vegetable broth are enhanced by the nutty quinoa and green edamame, giving it a unique taste.

Serving: 4-6 | Preparation Time: 10 minutes | Ready Time: 30 minutes

Ingredients:
- 1 tablespoon olive oil
- 1 chopped onion
- 2 cloves minced garlic
- 1 1/2 cups chopped carrots
- 2 cups vegetable broth
- 2 cups cooked quinoa
- 1/2 cup cooked edamame
- 1 (14.5-ounce) can diced tomatoes
- 1 teaspoon dried oregano
- 1/4 teaspoon ground black pepper
- 2 cups baby spinach

Instructions:
1. Heat the oil in a large pot over medium-high heat.
2. Add the onion and garlic and cook until they start to brown, about 5 minutes.
3. Stir in the carrots, vegetable broth, quinoa, edamame, tomatoes, oregano, and ground black pepper.
4. Bring the soup to a boil, then reduce the heat to low and simmer for 15 minutes.
5. Add the baby spinach and cook until wilted.

Nutrition Information:
Per serving, Quinoa and Edamame Minestrone Soup provides 118 Calories, 4.3 g Protein, 11.3 g Carbohydrates, 5.3 g Dietary Fiber, 13.3 g Fat, 2.3 g Saturated Fat, 2.5 g Sodium.

48. Pinto Bean and Barley Minestrone Soup

This delicious Pinto Bean and Barley Minestrone Soup is a hearty and comforting way to warm up. Packed with protein and fiber, this easy-to-make soup is a great way to warm up on cold days.

Serving: Makes 4-6 servings | Preparation Time: 15 minutes | Ready Time: 1 hour

Ingredients:
- 1 tablespoon olive oil
- 1 onion, diced
- 3 cloves garlic, minced
- 2 cups vegetable stock
- 2 (14.5 ounce) cans diced tomatoes
- 1 (14.5 ounce) can pinto beans, drained and rinsed
- 1/2 cup pearled barley
- 2 carrots, diced
- 2 celery stalks, diced
- 1 teaspoon dried parsley
- 1 teaspoon dried basil
- 1/4 teaspoon dried oregano
- Salt and freshly ground black pepper, to taste

Instructions:
1. Heat olive oil in a large pot or Dutch oven over medium heat. Add onion and garlic, and cook, stirring occasionally, until onions are translucent and garlic is fragrant, about 5 minutes.
2. Add vegetable stock, tomatoes, pinto beans, barley, carrots, celery, parsley, basil, oregano, and season with salt and pepper. Bring to a boil, then reduce heat and simmer, stirring occasionally, until vegetables are tender and soup has thickened, about 45 minutes.
3. Serve warm.

Nutrition Information: (per serving)
193 calories, 5g fat, 31g carbohydrates, 8g protein

49. Swiss Chard and Bean Minestrone Soup

Introducing a deliciously comforting and healthy bowl of Swiss Chard &
Bean Minestrone Soup that can be prepared in less than 30 minutes. It is
packed with flavour, nutrients, and protein!

Serving: 6-8 | Preparation Time: 15 minutes | Ready Time: 30 minutes

Ingredients:
- 2 tablespoons of olive oil
- 4 cloves of garlic, minced
- 1 onion, chopped
- 1 teaspoon of sea salt
- 2 potatoes, peeled and diced
- 2 stalks of celery, diced
- 2 large carrots, peeled and diced
- 8 cups of vegetable broth
- 2 cups of cooked cannellini beans
- 3 cups of chopped Swiss chard, packed
- 2 tablespoons of lemon juice
- 2 tablespoons of chopped fresh parsley

Instructions:
1. Heat olive oil in a large pot or Dutch oven over medium heat.
2. Add garlic, onion, and sea salt and cook until onion is softened, about
5 minutes.
3. Add potatoes, celery, and carrots. Cook for 5 minutes and stir
occasionally.
4. Pour in the vegetable broth and bring to a boil.
5. Reduce heat to a simmer, add in cannellini beans, Swiss chard, and
lemon juice. Simmer for 10 minutes.
6. Serve the soup warm with fresh parsley and enjoy!

Nutrition Information:
One serving (1/8 of total recipe) contains about 241 calories, 6.4g fat,
38.6g carbohydrates, 7g fiber, and 11.8g protein.

50. Couscous and Tomato Minestrone Soup

Intor: This hearty and comforting Minestrone soup is loaded with Mediterranean flavors from couscous and tomatoes. It's full of protein, perfect for a light dinner or a quick lunch.

Serving: Makes about 5 cups | Preparation Time: 10 minutes | Ready Time: 40 minutes

Ingredients:
- 2 tablespoons olive oil
- 1 onion, diced
- 2 carrots, diced
- 2 celery stalks, diced
- 2 garlic cloves, minced
- 2 tablespoons tomato paste
- 4 cups vegetable stock
- 1 can (14.5 ounces) diced tomatoes
- 1 teaspoon dried oregano
- 1/2 teaspoon dried thyme
- 2 bay leaves
- 1/2 cup dry couscous
- 2 tablespoons freshly chopped parsley
- Salt and pepper to taste

Instructions:
1. Heat the olive oil in a large pot over medium heat. Add the onion, carrots, celery, and garlic and cook for about 5 minutes, stirring occasionally, until vegetables are beginning to soften.
2. Add the tomato paste and cook for 1 more minute.
3. Add the vegetable stock, diced tomatoes, oregano, thyme, and bay leaves. Bring to a boil, then reduce heat to low and simmer for 25 minutes.
4. Add the couscous, parsley and season with salt and pepper to taste. Simmer for 5 more minutes.
5. Serve warm.

Nutrition Information:
Per serving: 134 calories, 6g fat, 20g carbohydrates, 3g protein

51. Parmesan and Mushroom Minestrone Soup

This delicious Parmesan and Mushroom Minestrone Soup is the perfect comfort dish to warm you up on a cold night. With a variety of vegetables and cheese, it comes together easily and can be served either as a starter or main dish.

Serving: 4 | Preparation Time: 20 minutes | Ready Time: 45 minutes

Ingredients:
- 2 tablespoons olive oil
- 1 onion, minced
- 2 garlic cloves, minced
- 2 carrots, peeled and diced
- 2 celery stalks, diced
- 1 zucchini, diced
- 1 yellow squash, diced
- 4 cups vegetable broth
- 1 can (14.5 oz) diced tomatoes
- 2 tablespoons tomato paste
- 2 tablespoons fresh oregano, finely chopped
- 1 teaspoon ground black pepper
- 1/2 teaspoon salt
- 1/4 pound fresh mushrooms, diced
- 1 cup ditalini or other small pasta
- 1 cup frozen green beans
- 1/2 cup shredded Parmesan cheese

Instructions:
1. Heat the oil in a large soup pot over medium heat. Add the onion and garlic and cook, stirring frequently, until onion is softened and fragrant, about 5 minutes.
2. Add the carrots, celery, zucchini, yellow squash, and mushrooms, and cook until veggies are soft, about 5 minutes.

3. Add the vegetable broth, tomatoes, tomato paste, oregano, pepper, and salt. Bring soup to a boil, then reduce heat and simmer for 25 minutes.

4. Add the pasta and green beans and simmer for 15 more minutes, or until pasta is cooked. Taste and adjust seasoning if needed.

5. Serve soup topped with Parmesan cheese.

Nutrition Information:
Calories: 212, Fat: 8.3g, Carbohydrates: 25.4g, Protein: 8.4g, Sodium: 707mg

52. Black Bean and Asparagus Minestrone Soup

This Black Bean and Asparagus Minestrone Soup is a vegan-friendly dish that is perfect for cold weather. Bursting with flavors from freshly cooked beans, asparagus and an assortment of spices, this recipe will bring warmth to your kitchen.

Serving: 4 – 6 servings | Preparation Time: 10 minutes | Ready Time: 45 minutes

Ingredients:
-1 tablespoon olive oil
-1 onion, diced
-3 cloves of garlic, minced
-1 can (14.5 oz) black beans, drained and rinsed
-1 can (14.5 oz) diced tomatoes
-2 cups vegetable broth
-2 cups water
-1 cup uncooked small pasta
-1/2 teaspoon Italian seasoning blend
-1/4 teaspoon ground black pepper
-1/4 teaspoon salt
-3 cups (1/2 lb) asparagus stalks, diced
-2 tablespoons chopped flat leaf parsley
-Grated parmesan cheese for garnish (optional)

Instructions:

1. Heat the olive oil in a large soup pot over medium-high heat.
2. Add the onion and garlic, cooking for 2-3 minutes or until onion is translucent.
3. Add the black beans, diced tomatoes, vegetable broth, water and pasta.
4. Stir in the Italian seasoning, black pepper and salt.
5. Bring to a boil and reduce time to medium-low, stirring occasionally.
6. Cover and simmer for 20 minutes.
7. Add the asparagus and cook for an additional 10 minutes until pasta is cooked and asparagus is tender.
8. Stir in the parsley and remove from heat.
9. Garnish with grated parmesan cheese.

Nutrition Information:
Serving Size: 1 serving, Calories: 181, Fat: 4 g, Carbohydrates: 31 g, Protein: 8 g

53. Tortellini and Spinach Minestrone Soup

Tortellini and Spinach Minestrone Soup is a hearty and delicious Italian-style soup that is perfect for colder weather. It's loaded up with vegetables, cheese tortellini and has a rich chicken broth base that is sure to fill you up.

Serving: 4-6 people | Preparation Time: 15 minutes | Ready Time: 45 minutes

Ingredients:
- 2 tablespoons olive oil
- 1 small onion, diced
- 2 cloves garlic, minced
- 2 carrots, peeled and diced
- 2 celery stalks, diced
- 2 cans (14.5 ounces each) low-sodium chicken broth
- 1 can (14.5 ounces) tomato sauce
- 1 can (15 ounces) white beans, drained
- 1 teaspoon dried oregano
- 1/2 teaspoon dried basil
- Salt and freshly ground black pepper, to taste

- 8 ounces cheese tortellini
- 2 cups baby spinach

Instructions:
1. Heat olive oil in a large pot over medium heat.
2. Add onion, garlic, carrots and celery and cook, stirring, until softened.
3. Add chicken broth, tomato sauce, beans, oregano, basil, and season with salt and pepper.
4. Bring to a simmer and cook for 15 minutes.
5. Add tortellini and spinach and cook for an additional 20-30 minutes or until the tortellini is cooked.
6. Serve warm and enjoy!

Nutrition Information (per serving):
641 calories, 28g fat, 73g carbohydrates, 32g protein.

54. Barley and Chicken Minestrone Soup

Barley and Chicken Minestrone Soup is a hearty and delicious one-pot vegetarian meal filled with vegetables, chicken and barley simmered in a savory broth. This easy soup makes a wonderful weeknight meal and can be served as either a main course or side dish.

Serving: 6 | Preparation Time: 15 minutes | Ready Time: 25 minutes

Ingredients:
- 2 tablespoons extra-virgin olive oil
- 1 small yellow onion, diced
- 2 cloves garlic, minced
- 2 carrots, diced
- 2 celery stalks, diced
- 1 teaspoon dried thyme
- 2 cups cooked diced chicken
- 1 can diced tomatoes
- 4 cups vegetable or chicken broth
- 1/4cup pearl barley
- 1 zucchini or summer squash, diced
- 1 cup frozen corn kernels

- 2 tablespoons chopped fresh flat-leaf parsley
- Salt and freshly ground black pepper to taste

Instructions:
1. Heat the olive oil in a large pot over medium heat. Add the onion and garlic and sauté until the vegetables are softened, about 4 minutes.
2. Add the carrots, celery, and dried thyme. Season with salt and pepper to taste and cook until the vegetables are slightly softened, about 4 minutes more.
3. Add the chicken, tomatoes, broth, and barley. Increase the heat to high and bring the mixture to a boil. Once boiling, reduce the heat to low, cover, and simmer for 15 minutes.
4. Add the zucchini and corn and cook for an additional 5 minutes, or until the barley is tender.
5. Remove from the heat and stir in the parsley. Taste and adjust seasoning with salt and pepper if desired.

Nutrition Information:
Calories: 309, Carbohydrates: 33g, Protein: 21g, Fat: 12g, Saturated Fat: 3g, Cholesterol: 64mg, Sodium: 819mg, Potassium: 845mg, Fiber: 6g, Sugar: 10g, Vitamin A: 3784IU, Vitamin C: 14mg, Calcium: 45mg, Iron: 2mg

55. Ricotta and Eggplant Minestrone Soup

This Ricotta and Eggplant Minestrone Soup is a hearty and flavorful take on the classic Italian soup. It's loaded with summer vegetables, creamy ricotta cheese and the perfect blend of herbs and spices for a delicious combination you won't soon forget!

Serving: 8 | Preparation Time: 10 minutes | Ready Time: 25 minutes

Ingredients:
- 2 tablespoons olive oil
- 1/2 cup diced onion
- 2 cloves garlic, mashed
- 1/2 teaspoon oregano
- 1 tablespoon tomato paste

- 1 medium eggplant, peeled and diced
- 4 cups vegetable broth
- 1 cup cooked cannellini beans
- 1 cup diced tomatoes
- 1 cup julienned carrots
- 1/4 cup chopped fresh parsley
- 2 tablespoons chopped chives
- 1/4 teaspoon chili flakes
- 2 tablespoons ricotta cheese
- Salt and pepper to taste

Instructions:

1. Heat the olive oil in a large soup pot over medium heat. Add the onion and garlic and sauté until the onion is translucent, about 5 minutes.
2. Add the oregano and tomato paste and cook, stirring occasionally, for 2 minutes.
3. Add the eggplant and vegetable broth and bring to a boil. Reduce the heat to low and simmer for 10 minutes.
4. Add the beans, tomatoes, carrots, parsley, chives, chili flakes, and ricotta. Simmer for 10 minutes more.
5. Season with salt and pepper to taste and serve hot.

Nutrition Information:

Serving size: 1 cup, Calories: 140; Total Fat: 6g; Saturated Fat: 1.5g; Cholesterol: 4g; Sodium: 590 mg; Total Carbohydrates: 17g; Dietary Fiber: 5g; Sugars: 5g; Protein: 7g

56. White Bean and Fennel Minestrone Soup

White Bean and Fennel Minestrone Soup is a hearty and comforting soup that is full of flavor. Perfect for a cold winter day, this soup is a great way to make a nutrient-dense meal.

Serving: 6 | Preparation Time: 15 minutes | Ready Time: 45 minutes

Ingredients:

- 2 tablespoons extra-virgin olive oil
- 1 large onion, chopped
- 2 cloves garlic, minced
- 1 large fennel bulb, chopped
- 4 cups vegetable broth
- 2 cans (14.5 ounces each) diced tomatoes
- 2 cups cooked white beans (or 1 can, rinsed and drained)
- 2 cups frozen cut green beans
- 1/4 cup small pasta (such as shells or ditalini)
- 2 tablespoons chopped fresh parsley
- 2 teaspoons dried oregano
- 1 teaspoon freshly ground black pepper
- 1/4 teaspoon salt

Instructions:
1. Heat the olive oil in a large pot over medium heat.
2. Add the onion and garlic, and cook until softened, about 4 minutes.
3. Add the fennel and cook for 5 minutes.
4. Add the broth, tomatoes, white beans, green beans, pasta, parsley, oregano, pepper, and salt to the pot.
5. Bring to a boil and reduce the heat to low.
6. Simmer for 30 minutes, until the vegetables are tender and the flavors have blended.

Nutrition Information:
Serving Size: 1 bowl, Calories: 308 , Total Fat: 6.6 g, Saturated Fat: 0.9 g, Cholesterol: 0 mg, Sodium: 488 mg, Total Carbohydrate: 49 g, Dietary Fiber: 14.4 g, Sugar: 8.5 g, Protein: 15.4 g

57. Squash and Pea Minestrone Soup

Squash and Pea Minestrone Soup is a delicious vegetable soup that is perfect for any season. It's hearty, healthy and packed with flavor. This vegan and gluten-free soup comes together quickly and easily and makes for a delicious lunch or dinner.

Serving: 6-8 | Preparation Time: 15 minutes | Ready Time: 30 minutes

Ingredients:

- 2 tablespoons olive oil
- 1 onion, diced
- 3 cloves garlic, minced
- 1 teaspoon dried oregano
- 1 teaspoon dried thyme
- 2 teaspoons sea salt
- 2 tablespoons tomato paste
- 5 cups vegetable broth
- 1 (15 ounce) can diced tomatoes
- 1 cup small diced butternut squash
- 1 (15 ounce) can chickpeas, drained and rinsed
- 1 cups frozen green peas
- 1 (15 ounce) can red kidney beans, drained and rinsed
- 2 tablespoons red wine vinegar

Instructions:

1. Heat olive oil in a pot over medium heat. Add onion and cook for about 3 minutes until soft.
2. Add garlic, oregano, thyme, salt, and tomato paste, and cook for another minute.
3. Add in the broth, diced tomatoes and squash and stir to combine. Bring soup to a boil, then reduce the heat and simmer for 10 minutes.
4. Add in chickpeas, peas and beans, and simmer for another 10 minutes or until the squash is tender.
5. Stir in the red wine vinegar and season with additional salt as needed.

Nutrition Information:

Calories – 160 , Fat – 6g, Carbohydrates – 21g, Protein – 7g, Fiber – 5g, Sugar – 5g

58. Orzo and Cauliflower Minestrone Soup

Orzo and Cauliflower Minestrone Soup is a wholesome and hearty vegetarian soup made with simple ingredients like orzo, cauliflower, and fire-roasted tomatoes. This soup is oil-free, packed with plant-based proteins and fiber, and is perfect for a quick and easy weeknight meal.

Serving: 4-6 | Preparation Time: 10 minutes | Ready Time: 25 minutes

Ingredients:
- 2 tablespoons vegetable stock or broth
- 1 medium onion, diced
- 2 garlic cloves, minced
- 1 teaspoon dried oregano
- 1/2 teaspoon red pepper flakes (optional)
- 1 large head of cauliflower, chopped into 1-inch florets
- 4 cups vegetable stock or broth (if using cubes, you will need 8 cubes)
- 1 28-ounce can fire-roasted diced tomatoes
- 1/2 cup orzo
- 1/2 teaspoon each sea salt and pepper
- 1/2 cup grated parmesan cheese, divided
- Chopped parsley, optional, for garnish

Instructions:
1. In a large pot, heat the vegetables stock or broth over medium heat. Add the onion and garlic and cook until softened, about 3 minutes.
2. Add the oregano, red pepper flakes, and cauliflower and cook for about 2 minutes.
3. Pour in the vegetable stock or broth and bring to a boil. Add the diced tomatoes, orzo, and season with sea salt and pepper. Reduce the heat to low and simmer for about 15 minutes, or until the cauliflower is tender and the orzo is cooked through.
4. Remove from heat and stir in 1/4 cup of the parmesan cheese. Serve in bowls, topped with remaining parmesan cheese and parsley (optional).

Nutrition Information (Per Serving):
Calories: 181, Carbs: 24g, Protein: 8g, Fat: 4g

59. Rice and Arugula Minestrone Soup

Rice and Arugula Minestrone Soup is a hearty, flavorful soup that is sure to be a hit with everyone. Rich with vegetables and packed with protein, this mix of classic minestrone flavors and fresh and nutritious arugula makes for a delicious and healthy soup.

Serving: 6-8 | Preparation Time: 10 minutes | Ready Time: 45 minutes

Ingredients:
- 2 tablespoons olive oil
- 1 small yellow onion, diced
- 1 celery stalk, diced
- 1/2 teaspoon dried oregano
- Salt and freshly ground pepper
- 2 large carrots, diced
- 1 Bay leaf
- 2 cloves garlic, minced
- 4 cups vegetable broth
- 1 can (15 ounces) can diced tomatoes
- 1 can (15 ounces) can white beans, drained and rinsed
- 1 cup white Arborio rice
- 2 cups fresh arugula, washed and chopped
- 2 tablespoons chopped fresh parsley

Instructions:
1. Heat the olive oil in a large soup pot over medium heat. Add the onion, celery, oregano, and a pinch each of salt and pepper and cook, stirring occasionally, until the vegetables are softened, about 5 minutes.
2. Add the carrots, bay leaf, and garlic, and cook for 2 minutes more.
3. Pour in the vegetable broth and diced tomatoes, and bring the soup to a boil. Stir in the beans and rice, reduce the heat, and simmer, uncovered, until the vegetables are tender and the rice is cooked, about 30 minutes.
4. Once cooked, stir in the arugula and parsley and cook for a few minutes more until wilted.

Nutrition Information:
Serving Size: 1 cup, Calories: 171, Total Fat: 4 g, Saturated Fat: 0.6 g, Carbohydrates: 27 g, Protein: 6.2 g, Fiber: 5 g, Sodium: 236 mg

60. Potato and Kale Minestrone Soup

This hearty and flavorful Potato and Kale Minestrone Soup is a delicious yet easy-to-prepare dinner option. Full of nourishing vegetables and warm, savory flavors, it's sure to satisfy any appetite.

Serving: 8 | Preparation Time: 10 minutes | Ready Time: 45 minutes

Ingredients:
- 2 tablespoons olive oil
- 1 onion, diced
- 2 cloves garlic, minced
- 2 carrots, diced
- 2 celery stalks, diced
- 2 teaspoons Italian seasoning
- 6 cups vegetable broth
- 3 potatoes, peeled and diced
- 2 (14-ounce) cans diced tomatoes
- 1 (14-ounce) can white kidney beans, drained and rinsed
- 1 cup kale, chopped
- Salt and pepper, to taste

Instructions:
1. Heat the olive oil in a large stockpot over medium heat.
2. Add the onion, garlic, carrots and celery to the pot and cook, stirring occasionally, until softened, about 3 minutes.
3. Add the Italian seasoning, vegetable broth, potatoes and diced tomatoes to the pot and bring to a simmer.
4. Cook for 20 minutes.
5. Add the white beans, kale, salt and pepper to the pot, stirring to combine.
6. Cook for an additional 15 minutes, or until potatoes and kale are tender.

Nutrition Information:
Calories: 247, Fat: 4.6g, Saturated fat: 0.6g, Carbohydrates: 42.4g, Protein: 10.4g, Cholesterol: 0mg, Sodium: 677mg, Fiber: 8.2g, Sugar: 5.2g

61. Spicy Red Lentil Minestrone Soup

This Spicy Red Lentil Minestrone Soup is a flavorful, hearty, and comforting one-pot meal! It's made with an aromatic blend of spices and vegetables, as well as red lentils and other protein sources to provide a nutritious and filling soup.

Serving: This recipe makes 4-6 servings | Preparation Time: This recipe takes 10 minutes to prepare | Ready Time: The soup will be ready to enjoy in 30 minutes.

Ingredients:
- 2 tablespoons olive oil;
-1 large onion, diced;
-3 cloves garlic, minced;
-1 teaspoon ground cumin;
-1 teaspoon chili powder;
- Salt, to taste;
- 3 carrots, peeled and diced;
-1 red bell pepper, diced;
-1 28- ounce can diced tomatoes;
-2 cups vegetable broth;
-1 cup dry red lentils;
-1/4 cup fresh parsley, chopped.

Instructions:
1. Heat the olive oil in a large soup pot over medium-high heat.
2. Add the onion and garlic and cook until onion is softened, about 3 minutes.
3. Add the cumin, chili powder, and salt, and cook for another 2 minutes.
4. Add the carrots, bell pepper, tomatoes, vegetable broth, and lentils. Stir until combined.
5. Bring to a boil, reduce heat to a simmer, and cook for 20 minutes or until the lentils and vegetables are tender.
6. Stir in the parsley and season with additional salt, if desired.
7. Serve hot.

Nutrition Information:
Each serving contains about 261 calories, 12 g fat, 36 g carbohydrates, and 8 g protein.

62. Chickpea and Leek Minestrone Soup

Chickpea and Leek Minestrone Soup is a vegetarian soup that is hearty and filling. This flavorful combination of chickpea, leeks, and vegetables is simmered in a light broth, creating a soup that is nourishing and comforting.

Serving: 4 | Preparation Time: 15 minutes | Ready Time: 40 minutes

Ingredients:
- 2 tablespoons olive oil
- 1 leek, roughly chopped
- 1 onion, chopped
- 2 carrots, peeled and diced
- 2 celery ribs, diced
- 4 cloves garlic, minced
- 1 teaspoon dried oregano
- 1 teaspoon dried thyme
- 6 cups vegetable broth
- 2 cups cooked chickpeas
- 1 potato, peeled and diced
- 2 tablespoons tomato paste
- 1 zucchini, diced
- 1 cup of fresh green beans, cut into 1-inch pieces
- 1 cup fresh spinach leaves, roughly chopped
- Sea salt and cracked black pepper, to taste

Instructions:
1. Heat the olive oil in a large soup pot or Dutch oven over medium heat.
2. Add the leek, onion, carrots, and celery, and sauté for 5-7 minutes until the vegetables are softened and fragrant.
3. Add the garlic, oregano, and thyme, and sauté for an additional minute.
4. Add the vegetable broth, chickpeas, potato, tomato paste, and zucchini, and bring to a boil.

5. Reduce the heat to low and simmer for 20-30 minutes, until the vegetables are tender.
6. Add the green beans and spinach and simmer for an additional 5 minutes.
7. Taste and season with salt and pepper.
8. Serve hot.

Nutrition Information:
Serving Size: 1 bowl (241g), Calories: 186, Fat: 7g, Carbohydrates: 25g, Protein: 8g, Sodium: 790mg, Fiber: 8g, Sugar: 5g

63. White Bean and Spinach Minestrone Soup

A warm and comforting dish, White Bean and Spinach Minestrone Soup is a delicious and nourishing meal that is sure to please. Packed with zesty flavors, this one-pot soup is easy to make and is perfect for sharing with family and friends.

Serving: 6-8 | Preparation Time: 10 minutes | Ready Time: 35 minutes

Ingredients:
- 2 tablespoons olive oil
- 1 small yellow onion, diced
- 2 cloves of garlic, minced
- 2 stalks of celery, diced
- 2 carrots, diced
- 8 cups vegetable stock
- 2 (14.5-ounce) cans white beans, drained and rinsed
- 1 (14.5-ounce) can diced tomatoes
- 1 teaspoon dried basil
- 1 teaspoon dried oregano
- 1 teaspoon dried thyme
- 1/2 teaspoon black pepper
- 2 (6-ounce) packages fresh baby spinach

Instructions:
1. Heat the olive oil in a large pot over medium heat.

2. Add the onion, garlic, celery, and carrots, and cook until the vegetables are softened, about 5 minutes.
3. Pour in the vegetable stock, white beans, diced tomatoes, basil, oregano, thyme, and black pepper.
4. Bring the soup to a boil, lower the heat to low, and simmer for 20 minutes.
5. Add the spinach to the soup and stir until wilted.

Nutrition Information:
Calories: 320, Total Fat: 5g, Saturated Fat: 0.5g, Cholesterol: 0mg, Total Carbohydrates: 49g, Dietary Fiber: 12g, Protein: 17g, Sodium: 1060mg

64. Tomato and Rice Minestrone Soup

Tomato and Rice Minestrone Soup is a hearty and flavorful Italian soup that is easily one of the most comforting soups out there. The fresh vegetables, tomatoes, broth, and rice combine to make a delicious and filling meal.

Serving: 4-6 | Preparation Time 15 mins | Ready in 45 mins.

Ingredients:
- 2 tablespoons olive oil
- 1 red onion, diced
- 1 carrot, diced
- 1 stalk of celery, diced
- 2 cloves of garlic, minced
- 2 large tomatoes, peeled and diced
- 1 cup uncooked white rice
- A bay leaf
- 2 cups vegetable or chicken broth
- 1/2 pound green beans, trimmed and cut into 1-inch pieces
- Salt and pepper to season

Instructions:
1. Heat the olive oil over medium heat in a large, heavy-bottom soup pot.
2. Add onion, carrot, celery, garlic, tomatoes and bay leaf. Cook until vegetables are softened and lightly browned, about 15 minutes.

3. Add the rice, vegetable or chicken broth, green beans, and a pinch of salt and pepper; bring just to a simmer.
4. Reduce heat, cover and simmer for 25 minutes.
5. Serve hot.

Nutrition Information:
Serving Size: 1 cup, Calories: 145 kcal, Total Fat: 4 g, Carbohydrates: 21 g, Protein: 4 g, Sodium: 550 mg

65. Bacon and Bean Minestrone Soup

My Bacon and Bean Minestrone Soup is an easy and comforting soup that's packed with vegetables, beans, and bacon for a comforting, delicious meal.

Serving: 6 | Preparation Time: 15 minutes | Ready Time: 45 minutes

Ingredients:
- 8 ounces bacon, chopped
- 2 garlic cloves, minced
- 1 large onion, chopped
- 2 large carrots, peeled & diced
- 2 celery stalks, diced
- 1/4 teaspoon red pepper flakes
- 4 cups low-sodium vegetable broth
- 2 medium potatoes, diced
- 1 teaspoon dried basil
- 1 teaspoon dried oregano
- 2 15-ounce cans cannellini beans, drained & rinsed
- 2 cups small soup pasta
- 2 large handfuls fresh spinach
- 2 tablespoons chopped fresh parsley

Instructions:
1. In a large soup pot, cook bacon over medium heat until it is almost crispy.
2. Add in the garlic, onion, carrots, celery, and red pepper flakes. Cook for 5 minutes, stirring occasionally.

3. Add in the vegetable broth, potatoes, and dried herbs. Increase the heat and bring the soup to a boil and reduce to a simmer for 15 minutes.
4. Add in the cannellini beans, pasta, and spinach. Cook for an additional 15 minutes or until the pasta is cooked through and the soup is thickened.
5. Serve the soup and garnish with fresh parsley.

Nutrition Information (per serving):
Calories: 350; Total Fat: 8.3g; Cholesterol: 27mg; Total Carbohydrate: 48.1g; Protein: 21.2g

66. Roasted Garlic and Mushroom Minestrone Soup

Roasted Garlic and Mushroom Minestrone Soup is a hearty and flavorful combination of roasted garlic and mushrooms, pastina and white beans simmered in a rich vegetable broth. It's a healthy, delicious and comforting meal, perfect for anytime of the year!

Serving: 6 | Preparation Time: 15 minutes | Ready Time: 45 minutes

Ingredients:
- 2-3 tablespoons extra-virgin olive oil
- 1 head of garlic
- 1 pound of mushrooms, sliced
- 2 celery stalks, diced
- 2 carrots, diced
- 1 onion, diced
- 6 cups vegetable broth
- 1 can diced tomatoes
- 2 cups cooked small pasta (such as orzo, pastina or ditalini)
- 1 cup white beans, cooked or canned
- Salt and pepper to taste
- 2 tablespoons chopped fresh parsley
- Parmesan cheese, grated (optional)

Instructions:
1. Preheat your oven to 375F (190°C).

2. Cut the top off the head of garlic, wrap it in foil, and bake for about 30 minutes.

3. Heat the olive oil in a large soup pot over medium-high heat. Add the mushrooms, celery, carrots and onion and sauté for 5-6 minutes, stirring occasionally.

4. Add the vegetable broth and tomatoes, bring to a boil, then reduce the heat and simmer for 15 minutes.

5. Meanwhile, carefully remove the garlic from the oven and allow to cool. Squeeze the roasted garlic out of its skins and add to the soup.

6. Add the cooked pasta and white beans to the soup, and simmer for another 10 minutes.

7. Season with salt and pepper to taste. Serve with a sprinkling of freshly chopped parsley and grated Parmesan cheese (optional).

Nutrition Information:
Per serving (1 bowl): 220 kcal, 8 g fat, 32 g carbohydrates, 5 g protein.

67. Polenta and Vegetable Minestrone Soup 68. Lentil and Carrot Minestrone Soup

This Lentil and Carrot Minestrone Soup is a deliciously comforting and nutritious meal featuring a hearty base of creamy polenta and a variety of veggies. Serve with a side of crusty bread for the perfect winter dinner.

Serving: 4-6 | Preparation Time: 15 minutes | Ready Time: 30 minutes

Ingredients:
-1/2 cup dry french green lentils
-2 tablespoons olive oil
-1 onion, diced
-2 carrots, diced
-2 cloves garlic, minced
-3/4 teaspoon kosher salt
-1/4 teaspoon freshly ground black pepper
-1 teaspoon dried oregano
-1 teaspoon dried basil
-1/2 teaspoon dried thyme
-1/2 fennel bulb, diced

-2 cups vegetable stock or broth
-1 (14-ounce) can diced tomatoes
-1/2 cup polenta
-1/4 cup freshly grated Parmesan cheese
-2 tablespoons chopped fresh parsley leaves

Instructions:
1. In a large soup pot, heat the olive oil over medium heat. Add in the onion and carrots and sauté for 2-3 minutes. Add the garlic, salt and pepper, oregano, basil, and thyme and sauté for 1 minute.
2. Add the lentils, fennel, vegetable stock and diced tomatoes to the pot and bring to a low simmer. Cook for 15 minutes until the lentils are cooked through.
3. Add the polenta to the pot and stir well. Cook for 5 minutes until the polenta is heated through.
4. Before serving, stir in the Parmesan cheese and parsley. Taste and adjust for additional seasoning, if desired.

Nutrition Information:
Calories: 280 kcal, Carbohydrates: 38 g, Protein: 12 g, Fat: 10 g, Saturated Fat: 2 g, Cholesterol: 5 mg, Sodium: 867 mg, Potassium: 592 mg, Fiber: 10 g, Sugar: 5 g, Vitamin A: 3515 IU, Vitamin C: 16 mg, Calcium: 98 mg, Iron: 4 mg

68. Butternut Squash and Lentil Minestrone Soup

Butternut Squash and Lentil Minestrone Soup is a deliciously hearty and warm soup that uses abundant vegetables and lentils. Perfect for vegetarian-friendly meals, this soup is easy to assemble and makes for a great meal.

Serving: 8 | Preparation Time: 20 minutes | Ready Time: 30 minutes

Ingredients:
- 2 tablespoons olive oil
- 1 onion, diced
- 2 cloves garlic, minced
- 2 medium carrots, diced

- 2 celery stalks, diced
- 1 teaspoon ground cumin
- 1 teaspoon dried oregano
- 4 cups vegetable broth
- 1 butternut squash, peeled and cubed
- 1 cup green lentils
- 1 can diced tomatoes, undrained
- 2 cups fresh baby spinach
- 1/4 cup fresh basil, chopped

Instructions:
1. Heat olive oil in a large stockpot over medium heat. Add the onion and garlic and cook, stirring frequently until lightly browned, about 4-5 minutes.
2. Add the carrots, celery, cumin and oregano and cook, stirring frequently until the vegetables are soft, about 3 minutes.
3. Add the vegetable broth, butternut squash, lentils and tomatoes and bring to a boil.
4. Reduce heat to low and let simmer for 20 minutes or until lentils are tender.
5. Add spinach and basil and simmer for an additional 2 minutes.

Nutrition Information:
Per serving: 180 calories, 8g fat, 22g carbohydrates, 5g protein, 6g fiber

69. Bacon and Cabbage Minestrone Soup

Bacon and Cabbage Minestrone Soup is a warm and comforting soup with the delicious flavors of bacon, cabbage, and mineral broth. It's a hearty, nourishing soup that's easy to make and perfect for a cold winter evening.

Serving: 4-6 | Preparation Time: 10 minutes | Ready Time: 30 minutes

Ingredients:
- 2 tablespoon olive oil
- 1/2 pound bacon, chopped
- 1 white onion, diced

- 4 cloves garlic, minced
- 2 sprigs rosemary
- 1 small head of cabbage, chopped
- 6 cups mineral or chicken broth
- 2 cans white beans, drained and rinsed
- 2 bay leaves
- 1 teaspoon sea salt
- 1/4 teaspoon black pepper

Instructions:
1. Heat the olive oil in a large pot over medium heat.
2. Add the bacon and onion to the pot and cook for about 5 minutes until the bacon is crisp.
3. Add the garlic, rosemary, and cabbage and cook for a few more minutes.
4. Pour in the broth and add the beans, bay leaves, salt and pepper.
5. Bring the soup to a boil, then reduce the heat to low and simmer for 15-20 minutes.
6. Remove the bay leaves and serve.

Nutrition Information:
Calories: 240, Fat: 8g, Carbs: 24g, Protein: 12g, Fiber: 6g, Sugar: 7g

70. Fennel and Barley Minestrone Soup

Fennel and Barley Minestrone Soup is a hearty, flavorful vegetable-filled soup perfect for a cold winter day. This delicious dish takes approximately 45 minutes to prepare and is ready to serve in one hour.

Serving: 4-6 | Preparation Time: 10 minutes | Ready Time: 1 hour

Ingredients:
- 2 tablespoons olive oil
- 2 cloves garlic, minced
- 1 red onion, chopped
- 2 fennel bulbs, cored and chopped
- 2 stalks celery, chopped
- 1 teaspoon dried oregano

- 1/2 teaspoon red pepper flakes
- 2 teaspoons kosher salt
- 1 teaspoon black pepper
- 2 cups vegetable broth
- 2 cups chopped tomatoes
- 2 cups diced potatoes
- 1 cup barley
- 1/2 cup frozen peas
- 1/2 cup grated Parmigiano-Reggiano cheese

Instructions:
1. Heat olive oil in a large pot over medium heat.
2. Add garlic, onion, fennel, celery, oregano, red pepper flakes, salt and pepper, and cook, stirring frequently, for 5 minutes.
3. Add vegetable broth, tomatoes, potatoes, and barley, and bring to a boil.
4. Reduce heat and simmer for 30 minutes.
5. Add peas and simmer for an additional 10 minutes.
6. Serve with grated Parmigiano-Reggiano cheese.

Nutrition Information:
Calories- 314, Fat- 6g, Carbohydrates- 58g, Protein- 9g

71. Italian Sausage and Sweet Potato Minestrone Soup

This hearty and flavorful Italian Sausage and Sweet Potato Minestrone Soup makes for a delicious and comforting meal. This soup is filled with sweet potatoes, Italian sausage, kidney beans, and vegetables, cooked in a rich vegetable broth.

Serving: 4-6 | Preparation Time: 10 minutes | Ready Time: 60 minutes

Ingredients:
- 1 tablespoon olive oil
- 1 large onion, diced
- 1 large sweet potato, peeled and diced
- 1 clove of garlic, chopped

- 1 teaspoon dried parsley
- 1 teaspoon dried oregano
- 1/4 teaspoon salt
- 1/2 teaspoon pepper
- 1 pound dried Italian Sausage, crumbled into small pieces
- 4 cups vegetable broth
- 1 cup canned diced tomatoes
- 1 (15.5 oz) can of kidney beans, rinsed and drained
- 4 - 6 cups fresh spinach leaves
- Parmesan cheese (optional)

Instructions:
1. Heat the olive oil in a large soup pot over medium heat. Add the onions, sweet potatoes, garlic, parsley, oregano, salt, and pepper. Cook while stirring, until the onions and sweet potatoes are softened, about 5 minutes.
2. Add the Italian sausage and cook for an additional 8-10 minutes, until the sausage is lightly browned.
3. Add the vegetable broth, tomatoes, and kidney beans. Bring the soup to a boil and then turn the heat down to low. Simmer for 25-30 minutes, until the sweet potatoes are soft.
4. Add the spinach leaves and cook for an additional 5 minutes.
5. Serve the soup warm with Parmesan cheese sprinkled on top, if desired.

Nutrition Information (Per Serving):
Calories: 381; Fat: 15.4g; Carbohydrates: 37.5g; Protein: 23.6g; Sodium: 912.6mg; Fiber: 9.7g.

72. Chorizo and Bean Minestrone Soup

Chorizo and Bean Minestrone Soup is a flavorful and hearty soup that combines chorizo sausage, kidney beans, and a wide range of vegetables in a rich tomato base. It is an easy dish to prepare, with a vibrant flavor that is perfect for any time of the year.

Serving: 8-10 | Preparation Time: 15 minutes | Ready Time: 1 hour

Ingredients:
- 2 tablespoons olive oil
- 1 onion, diced
- 2 garlic cloves, chopped
- 200 grams chorizo sausage, diced
- 1 red capsicum, diced
- 1 cup diced tomato
- 2 cups vegetable broth
- 1 cup red kidney beans
- 2 tablespoons tomato paste
- 2 teaspoons oregano
- 2 bay leaves
- 1/3 cup uncooked small pasta
- 2 zucchini, diced
- 2 carrots, diced

Instructions:
1. Heat the olive oil in a large pot over medium heat.
2. Add the onion and garlic and cook for 2 minutes, stirring occasionally.
3. Add the chorizo sausage and cook for 5 minutes, stirring occasionally.
4. Add the red capsicum, diced tomato, vegetable broth, kidney beans, tomato paste, oregano, and bay leaves.
5. Bring the mixture to a boil, reduce the heat to low, and simmer for 20 minutes.
6. Add the uncooked pasta, zucchini, and carrots and simmer for another 15 minutes.
7. Serve the soup warm and enjoy!

Nutrition Information:
Calories: 140; Total Fat: 7g; Saturated Fat: 2g; Cholesterol: 10mg; Sodium: 420mg; Total Carbohydrates: 13g; Dietary Fiber: 3g; Sugars: 3g; Protein: 6g.

73. Quinoa and Asparagus Minestrone Soup

This quinoa and asparagus minestrone soup is a light and flavorful veggie-packed meal option for any time of year. It's low in calories but big on nutrition.

Serving: 6-8 | Preparation Time: 10 minutes | Ready Time: 40 minutes

Ingredients:
- 1 Tbsp olive oil
- 1 cup onion, chopped
- 2 cloves garlic, minced
- 3 cups vegetable broth
- 1 cup quinoa, rinsed and drained
- 2 cups asparagus spears, chopped
- 1 (15-ounce) can diced tomatoes
- 1 (15-ounce) can white beans, drained
- 2 basil leaves, chopped
- Salt and pepper, to taste

Instructions:
1. Heat the olive oil in a large saucepan over medium-high heat.
2. Add the onion and garlic and sauté for 3 minutes.
3. Pour in the vegetable broth and quinoa. Bring to a boil, reduce the heat to low and simmer for 20 minutes.
4. Add the asparagus, tomatoes, beans, basil and salt and pepper to taste. Simmer for an additional 10 minutes.
5. Serve and enjoy.

Nutrition Information:
Serving: 1 (250 g) | Calories: 250 kcal | Carbohydrates: 34.3g | Protein: 11.3g | Fat: 6.6g | Saturated Fat: 1g | Sodium: 3 mg | Potassium: 477mg | Fiber: 9.7g | Sugar: 4.6g | Vitamin A: 10IU | Vitamin C: 10mg | Calcium: 118mg | Iron: 9mg

74. Split Pea and Parsley Minestrone Soup

This Split Pea and Parsley Minestrone Soup is fresh, savory, and satisfying. With a combination of split peas, vegetables, herbs and spices, this soup is a winner in any kitchen. Enjoy it as is, or add some of your favorite accompaniments.

Serving: 6-8 bowls | Preparation Time: 10 minutes | Ready Time: 40 minutes

Ingredients:
-2 tablespoons olive oil
-1 onion, chopped
-1 celery stalk, diced
-2 garlic cloves, minced
-1 large carrot, diced
-2 teaspoons diced fresh rosemary
-2 teaspoons dried oregano
-1 teaspoon dried basil
-1/2 teaspoon smoked paprika
-1 cup split peas, soaked overnight
-4 cups vegetable stock
-1 (14.5-ounce) can diced tomatoes
-1 bay leaf
-3 cups chopped kale
-1/2 cup chopped fresh parsley
-Salt and freshly ground pepper, to taste
-Grated Parmesan cheese, to serve (optional)

Instructions:
1. Heat the oil in a large pot over medium heat.
2. Add the onion, celery and garlic, and cook, stirring occasionally, until softened, about 5 minutes.
3. Add the carrot, rosemary, oregano, basil and smoked paprika, and cook for another 2 minutes.
4. Add the split peas and vegetable stock, and bring to a boil.
5. Reduce the heat to low and simmer for about 25 minutes, stirring occasionally.
6. Add the diced tomatoes, bay leaf and kale, and simmer for another 5 minutes.
7. Remove from heat and stir in the fresh parsley.
8. Season with salt and pepper, to taste.
9. Serve hot with grated Parmesan cheese, if desired.

Nutrition Information:
Calories: 240, Fat: 8 g, Carbohydrates: 33 g, Protein: 11 g, Fiber: 6 g

75. Roasted Vegetable and Rice Minestrone Soup

This delicious Roasted Vegetable and Rice Minestrone Soup is a hearty and healthy meal, perfect for busy weeknights. Made with a combination of aromatic vegetables, healthy grains and flavorful herbs, it is sure to please any crowd.

Serving: 6 | Preparation Time: 10 mins | Ready Time: 35 mins

Ingredients:
  - 2 tbsp olive oil
  - 1 onion, chopped
  - 2 cloves garlic, chopped
  - 1 red sweet pepper, chopped
  - 1 celery stalk, chopped
  - 1 zucchini, cubed
  - 2 large carrots, sliced
  - 2 cups of cooked brown rice
  - 2 cups vegetable broth
  - 2 cups canned diced tomatoes
  - 1/2 tsp dried oregano
  - 1/2 tsp dried thyme
  - 1/2 cup cooked green lentils
  - Salt and pepper to taste

Instructions:
1. Preheat the oven to 375F.
2. Spread the onion, garlic, red pepper, celery, zucchini and carrots onto a baking sheet and simmer in the preheated oven for around 20 minutes, stirring once or twice.
3. Heat the olive oil in a Dutch oven or soup pot over medium heat. Add the roasted vegetables and cook until tender.
4. Add the cooked brown rice, vegetable broth, diced tomatoes, oregano, thyme, and green lentils and bring the soup to a boil. Reduce the heat and simmer until the vegetables are tender, about 10 minutes.
5. Season with salt and pepper to taste and serve hot.

Nutrition Information (Per Serving):
Calories: 200; Total Fat: 5g; Saturated Fat: 1g; Carbohydrate: 30g; Fiber: 4g; Protein: 6g; Sodium: 210mg

76. Barley and Spinach Minestrone Soup

This Barley and Spinach Minestrone Soup is a delicious and healthy vegetarian meal that's packed full of veggie goodness and fiber.

Serving: 8 | Preparation Time: 15 mins | Ready Time: 30 mins

Ingredients:
- 1 tbsp olive oil
- 1 onion, diced
- 2 garlic cloves, minced
- 1 large carrot, diced
- 2 celery stalks, sliced
- 1 zucchini, diced
- 2 cups vegetable broth
- 1 (15 ounce) can diced tomatoes
- 2 cups cooked barley
- 1 (15 ounce) can cannellini beans, drained and rinsed
- 2 cups baby spinach leaves
- 2 tsp Italian seasoning
- Salt and pepper to taste

Instructions:
1. Heat olive oil in a large pot over medium heat.
2. Add onion, garlic, carrot, celery and zucchini. Cook for about 5–7 minutes, until onions are translucent.
3. Add vegetable broth, canned tomatoes, cooked barley, beans, spinach, Italian seasoning, and season with salt and pepper.
4. Bring to a boil, reduce heat to low and simmer for 15 minutes.

Nutrition Information (per serving):
Calories: 224, Total Fat 4g, Saturated Fat 1g, Cholesterol 0mg, Sodium 762mg, Carbohydrate 37g, Dietary Fiber 9g, Protein 8g.

77. Potato and Sausage Minestrone Soup

Potato and Sausage Minestrone Soup is a hearty, savory soup with potatoes, sausage, and vegetables in a fragrant tomato-based broth. It's the perfect comforting bowl to warm you up on a chilly day.

Serving: 6-8 | Preparation Time: 10 minutes | Ready Time: 40 minutes

Ingredients:
- 7 cups chicken broth
- 2 tablespoons olive oil
- 1 yellow onion, diced
- 2 cloves garlic, minced
- 2 cups diced potatoes
- 2 ripe tomatoes, diced, or 1 (14.5 oz) can fire-roasted diced tomatoes
- 1 cup diced carrots
- 4 cups chopped kale, chopped
- 4 ounces (1 link) Italian sausage, mild, casings removed
- 2 tablespoons tomato sauce
- 2 teaspoons Italian seasoning
- Salt and pepper, to taste

Instructions:
1. In a large stockpot, heat olive oil over medium-high heat.
2. Add onion and garlic and sauté for 3-4 minutes, until fragrant and softened.
3. Add potatoes and stir to coat in the oil.
4. Sauté for 5 minutes, stirring occasionally, until potatoes begin to brown.
5. Add chicken broth, diced tomatoes, carrots, kale, sausage, tomato sauce, Italian seasoning and salt and pepper.
6. Bring the mixture to a boil, reduce heat to low and simmer, stirring occasionally, for 30 minutes, or until vegetables are tender.
7. Serve hot with a side of crusty bread.

Nutrition Information: (Per Serving)
Calories: 217 kcal Carbohydrates: 21.6g, Protein: 12.2g, Fat: 9.2g, Saturated Fat: 2.3g, Sodium: 1453mg, Fiber: 4.4g, Sugar: 5.1g

78. Edamame and Kale Minestrone Soup

This flavorful soup combines the nutritional powerhouse veggies of edamame and kale with a rich tomato broth into a delectably warming minestrone.

Serving: 6-8 | Preparation Time: 15 minutes | Ready Time: 60 minutes

Ingredients:
- 2 tablespoons olive oil
- 1 small onion, diced
- 2 cloves garlic, minced
- 2 carrots, diced
- 2 celery stalks, diced
- 1 teaspoon dried oregano
- 1 teaspoon dried basil
- Salt and pepper to taste
- 3 cups vegetable broth
- 2 cans (14.5 ounces each) diced tomatoes
- 1 cup cooked edamame
- 8 ounces kale, stems removed and torn into bite-size pieces
- 2 tablespoons fresh parsley, chopped

Instructions:
1. Heat oil in a large pot over medium heat.
2. Add onions and garlic, cooking until fragrant. Stir in carrots and celery, sauteing for 5 minutes.
3. Add oregano, basil, salt, pepper, broth, and tomatoes to the pot. Bring to a boil, then reduce heat and simmer for 20 minutes.
4. Knead edamame, kale, and parsley into soup. Simmer for an additional 20 minutes.
5. Serve warm.

Nutrition Information (per serving):
Calories: 180, Total Fat: 5g, Cholesterol: 0mg, Sodium: 490mg, Carbohydrates: 24.5g, Dietary Fibre: 7g, Sugars: 8g, Protein: 12g.

79. Chickpea and Mushroom Minestrone Soup

Chickpea and Mushroom Minestrone Soup - This hearty and savory minestrone is full of comforting vegetables. It's easy to make and uses simple ingredients, making it a great choice for weeknight dinners.

Serving: Makes 6 servings | Preparation Time: 10 minutes | Ready Time: 25 minutes

Ingredients:
- 2 tablespoons olive oil
- 1 onion, small dice
- 2 carrots, small dice
- 2 celery stalks, small dice
- 1/4 teaspoon dried thyme
- 4 cloves garlic, minced
- 2 tablespoons tomato paste
- 4 cups vegetable broth
- 2 bay leaves
- 1 14.5-ounce can diced tomatoes
- 1 8-ounce can chickpeas, drained and rinsed
- 4 ounces mushrooms, sliced
- 2 cups cooked small pasta, such as ditalini
- 1 tablespoon chopped fresh basil
- 2 tablespoons chopped fresh Italian parsley
- Salt and freshly ground black pepper

Instructions:
1. Heat the oil in a large pot over medium-high heat.
Add the onions, carrots and celery, and cook until softened, about 5 minutes. Add the thyme, garlic and tomato paste and cook for a minute more.
2. Add the broth, bay leaves, tomatoes and chickpeas, and bring to a simmer. Reduce the heat to medium and cook for 15 minutes.
3. Add the mushrooms and pasta, and cook until the mushrooms are softened and the pasta is cooked, about 5 minutes.
4. Remove the bay leaves and season with salt and pepper, to taste. Stir in the basil and parsley and serve.

Nutrition Information:
Per Serving • Calories: 306 • Carbohydrates: 42g • Protein: 10g • Fat: 11g • Sodium: 819mg • Fiber: 8g • Sugar: 10g

80. Potato and Broccoli Minestrone Soup

Potato and Broccoli Minestrone Soup is an easy, healthy, and satisfying soup made with potatoes, broccoli, and vegetables in an herbed broth. This simple soup is perfect for chilly evenings and makes a great meal when served with a side salad and some crusty bread

Serving: 8 | Preparation Time: 15 minutes | Ready Time: 40 minutes

Ingredients:
- 3 tablespoons olive oil
- 1 onion, chopped
- 2 cloves garlic, minced
- 4 carrots, chopped
- 2 celery stalks, chopped
- 2 potatoes, peeled and diced
- 5 cups vegetable broth
- 1 cup canned diced tomatoes
- 2 cups chopped broccoli
- 1 teaspoon dried oregano
- 1 teaspoon dried basil
- Salt and pepper to taste

Instructions:
1. In a large soup pot, heat oil over medium-high heat and sauté onion, garlic, carrots, and celery for about 3 minutes, stirring occasionally.
2. Add potatoes, broth, tomatoes, broccoli, oregano, and basil to the pot. Bring to a boil, lower heat to medium-low, and simmer for 25 minutes, or until potatoes are tender.
3. Season with salt and pepper to taste, and serve.

Nutrition Information:

Calories: 147 kcal, Carbohydrates: 17 g, Protein: 5 g, Fat: 7 g, Saturated Fat: 1 g, Sodium: 1083 mg, Potassium: 550 mg, Fiber: 4 g, Sugar: 6 g, Vitamin A: 5288 IU, Vitamin C: 48 mg, Calcium: 73 mg, Iron: 2 mg

81. Red Lentil and Coconut Minestrone Soup

This vibrant and flavorful Red Lentil and Coconut Minestrone Soup is the perfect comfort food for cold winter days. Rich and creamy with small red lentils and coconut milk, this winning combination will warm your soul and keep you nourished.

Serving: Serves 8 | Preparation Time: 10 minutes | Ready time: 35 minutes

Ingredients
- 1 tablespoon of oil
- 1 onion, chopped
- 2 cloves of garlic, minced
- 2 carrots, diced
- 2 celery sticks, diced
- 2 teaspoons of ground cumin
- 1 teaspoon of ground coriander
- 1 teaspoon of chilli powder
- 1/2 teaspoon of paprika
- pinch of sea salt
- 400g can of chopped tomatoes
- 2 tablespoons of tomato paste
- 2.5 litres of vegetable stock
- 200g of red lentils
- 400ml can of coconut milk
- 2 tablespoons of chopped fresh parsley
- large handful of fresh spinach

Instructions -
1. Heat the oil in a large pan then add the chopped onion and the minced garlic, and cook until soft.

2. Add the diced carrots and celery, and stir.

3. Add the ground cumin, coriander, chilli powder and paprika and season with a pinch of salt.

4. Then add the chopped tomatoes, tomato paste, and vegetable stock and bring to a boil.

5. Add the red lentils, reduce the heat and simmer for 15 minutes.

6. Stir in the coconut milk and simmer for another 10 minutes.

7. Add the chopped parsley and spinach and stir until wilted.

8. Serve with a squeeze of lemon and a sprinkle of fresh parsley.

Nutrition Information
Per serving: Calories 243, Total Fat 9.1g, Sodium 617mg, Total Carbohydrates 31.7g, Dietary Fiber 6.9g, Protein 10.2g.

82. Black Bean and Red Pepper Minestrone Soup

This hearty Black Bean and Red Pepper Minestrone Soup is packed with dark red kidney beans, peppers, zucchini and a healthy helping of Italian herbs and spices. Perfect for a chilly day, this one-pot dish is filling, nutritious and incredibly flavorful.

Serving: 4 | Preparation Time: 10 minutes | Ready Time: 40 minutes

Ingredients:
- 2 tablespoons olive oil
- 1 red onion, chopped
- 2 cloves garlic, minced
- 2 teaspoons dried oregano
- 1 teaspoon dried basil
- 2 bell peppers, chopped
- 2 tablespoons tomato paste
- 4 cups vegetable broth
- 2 (15-ounce) cans dark red kidney beans, drained and rinsed
- 1 zucchini, chopped
- Salt and pepper, to taste
- 2 tablespoons freshly chopped parsley, for garnish

Instructions:
1. Heat oil in a large pot over medium-high heat. Add onion and garlic and cook, stirring occasionally, until tender and fragrant, about 5 minutes.
2. Add oregano, basil, bell peppers and tomato paste, season with salt and pepper and cook, stirring occasionally, until the bell peppers are softened, about 3 minutes.
3. Add broth, beans and zucchini. Bring to a boil, reduce heat to low and simmer, covered, for 20 minutes.
4. Ladle the soup into bowls and garnish with parsley.

Nutrition Information:
Calories: 225 per serving, Fat: 5g, Carbohydrates: 34g, Protein: 9g, Sodium: 26mg, Potassium: 426mg, Fiber: 9.4g, Sugar: 3.2g

83. Farro and Tomato Minestrone Soup

Farro and Tomato Minestrone Soup is a hearty and flavorful vegetarian soup. This one-pot meal is packed with fresh veggies and will leave your family feeling satisfied and nourished.

Serving: 4 | Preparation Time: 15 minutes | Ready Time: 40 minutes

Ingredients:
-2 tablespoons olive oil
-1 small onion, diced
-3 cloves garlic, minced
-2 cups tomato sauce
-2 cups vegetable broth
-2 cups water
-1 teaspoon oregano
-1 teaspoon basil
-1/2 teaspoon black pepper
-1/2 teaspoon red pepper flakes
-1/4 teaspoon salt
-1/2 cup uncooked farro, rinsed
-2 cups frozen mixed vegetables
-1 (15-ounce) can kidney beans, drained and rinsed

-2 tablespoons fresh parsley, chopped

Instructions:
1. Heat the olive oil in a large pot over medium-high heat.
2. Add the onion and garlic and cook until the onion is softened and fragrant, about 5 minutes.
3. Add the tomato sauce, vegetable broth, water, oregano, basil, black pepper, red pepper flakes, salt, and farro. Bring to a boil, then reduce heat to a simmer and cook, stirring occasionally, for 20 minutes.
4. Add the frozen vegetables and kidney beans and simmer another 10 minutes, or until the farro is tender.
5. Stir in the parsley and season to taste with additional salt and pepper, if desired.

Nutrition Information:
Calories: 226.9, Fat: 5.7 g, Carbohydrates: 34.8 g , Protein: 9.9 g, Fiber: 5.8 g

84. Quinoa and Chard Minestrone Soup

This Quinoa and Chard Minestrone Soup is a hearty and wholesome soup packed with vegetables and flavor. A delicious way to get your daily servings of vegetables.

Serving: 6-8 | Preparation Time: 10 minutes | Ready Time: 40 minutes

Ingredients:
- 2 tablespoons extra-virgin olive oil
- 1 medium yellow onion, small dice
- 2 carrots, small dice
- 2 celery stalks, small dice
- 2 cloves garlic, minced
- 2 (15 oz) cans diced tomatoes
- 1 (15 oz) can cannellini beans, drained and rinsed
- 2 cups vegetable broth
- 3 cups roughly chopped Swiss chard
- 1 cup uncooked quinoa, rinsed
- 1 teaspoon dried oregano

- 1/2 teaspoon smoked paprika
- 1/2 teaspoon ground turmeric
- Salt and freshly ground black pepper
- 1/4 cup chopped fresh parsley
- 1/4 cup grated Parmesan cheese, for topping

Instructions:
1. In a large pot, heat olive oil over medium heat. Add onion, carrots, and celery and cook, stirring occasionally, until vegetables have softened, about 5 minutes. Add garlic and cook until fragrant, 30 – 60 seconds.
2. Add tomatoes, beans, vegetable broth, Swiss chard, quinoa, oregano, paprika, and turmeric. Bring soup to a boil, reduce heat to low, and simmer, uncovered, until quinoa is cooked, about 30 minutes. Season to taste with salt and pepper.
3. Serve warm, topped with fresh parsley and Parmesan cheese.

Nutrition Information:
Serving size: 1/8 of total recipe, Calories: 177, Fat: 5g, Carbohydrates: 28g, Protein: 7g, Sodium: 309mg

85. Butternut Squash and Asparagus Minestrone Soup

Butternut squash and asparagus meld together into a delicious and comforting Minestrone soup in this easy one-pot meal.

Serving: 4 | Preparation Time: 10 mins | Ready Time: 20 mins

Ingredients:
- 2 tablespoons olive oil
- 1 red onion, diced
- 1 garlic clove, minced
- 2 medium carrots, sliced
- 2 celery stalks, diced
- 2 tablespoons fresh thyme, chopped
- 2 cups butternut squash, cubed
- 2 cups vegetable broth

- 1 cup asparagus, cut into 1-inch pieces
- 2 tablespoons tomato paste
- 2 15-oz cans of diced tomatoes
- 1 tablespoon of balsamic vinegar
- 1 15-oz can of white beans, drained
- Salt and pepper to taste

Instructions:
1. Heat the olive oil in a large stockpot over medium heat and add the diced onion. Sauté until the onion is soft and translucent, about 5 minutes.
2. Add the minced garlic, carrots, and celery to the pot and sauté for another few minutes until the vegetables start to soften and become fragrant.
3. Add the butternut squash and thyme to the pot and stir to combine.
4. Pour the vegetable stock into the pot and bring to a boil. Then reduce the heat to a simmer and add in the asparagus and tomato paste. Simmer for 10 minutes or until the vegetables are tender.
5. Add the diced tomatoes, balsamic vinegar, and white beans and simmer for another 10 minutes. Season with salt and pepper to taste.
6. To serve, ladle the soup into bowls and enjoy.

Nutrition Information:
188 calories per serving, 7.4g of fat, 27.2g of carbohydrates and 9.4g of protein.

86. White Bean and Carrot Minestrone Soup

This White Bean and Carrot Minestrone Soup is a hearty, nourishing soup that brings a healthy combination of vegetables, tomato, and white beans together for a delicious and nutritious meal. With the combination of all natural ingredients, this soup is sure to give you a fulfilling and energizing meal that's full of flavor.

Serving: 4-6 | Preparation Time: 10 minutes | Ready Time: 15 minutes

Ingredients:
-2 tablespoons olive oil

- 1 garlic clove, minced
- 2 medium carrots, diced
-1 medium onion, chopped
-2 celery sticks, diced
-1 teaspoon dried oregano
- 1 teaspoon salt
- 2 cups vegetable broth
- 1 (14-ounce) can diced tomatoes
-1 (14-ounce) can white beans, drained and rinsed
- freshly ground black pepper
-Chopped fresh basil, to garnish

Instructions:
1. Heat the olive oil in a large pot over medium heat. Sauté the garlic, carrots, onion, and celery until soft and fragrant, about 5 minutes.
2. Add the oregano, salt and vegetable broth, and stir. Bring to a boil, then reduce the heat to low and simmer for 10 minutes.
3. Add the tomatoes, white beans, and black pepper. Cook for another 5 minutes.
4. Garnish with fresh basil, if desired, and serve warm.

Nutrition Information:
Each serving of White Bean and Carrot Minestrone contains approximately 137 calories, 2.5g fat, 21g carbohydrate, 5.5g protein, 6g dietary fiber, and 347mg sodium.

87. Lentil and Spinach Minestrone Soup

Lentil and Spinach Minestrone Soup is a simple, delicious and nutritious soup that is perfect for lunch or dinner. This stew is a great way to use up veggies in the fridge, and thanks to the lentils, it's full of plant-based protein.

Serving: 8-10 servings | Preparation Time: 15 minutes | Ready Time: 30 minutes

Ingredients:
- 2 tablespoons olive oil

- 1 yellow onion, diced
- 3 cloves garlic, minced
- 1 teaspoon dried oregano
- 2 teaspoon ground cumin
- 4 cups vegetable broth
- 1 can (15 ounces) diced tomatoes
- 1 cup dry lentils
- 2 carrots, diced
- 2 stalks celery, diced
- 2 cups spinach, chopped
- salt and pepper to taste

Instruction:
1. Heat the olive oil in a large pot over medium-high heat.
2. Add the onion and garlic, and cook until softened, about 5 minutes.
3. Add the oregano and cumin, and cook for another minute.
4. Add the vegetable broth, diced tomatoes, lentils, carrots, and celery. Bring to a boil, then reduce the heat to medium-low and simmer for 20 minutes.
5. Add the spinach and season with salt and pepper to taste. Simmer for an additional 5 minutes.
6. Serve warm with a sprinkle of fresh parsley, if desired.

Nutrition Information:
Each serving contains approximately: 147 calories, 6g fat, 18g carbohydrates, 7g protein and 5g of dietary fiber.

88. Green Bean and Orzo Minestrone Soup

Green Bean and Orzo Minestrone Soup is a delicious, comforting vegan soup full of healthy vegetables and enriched with the flavors of herbs and spices.

Serving: 6 serving | Preparation Time: 10 minutes | Ready Time: 30 minutes

Ingredients:
- 2 tablespoons olive oil

- 2 cloves garlic, minced
- 1 onion, diced
- 2 carrots, diced
- 2 stalks celery, diced
- 2 potatoes, diced
- 8 ounces green beans, cut in half
- 1 teaspoon dried basil
- 1 teaspoon dried oregano
- 1 teaspoon dried thyme
- 4 cups vegetable broth
- 1 can (14.5 ounces) diced tomatoes
- 1 cup uncooked orzo
- Salt and pepper, to taste
- 2 tablespoons fresh parsley, chopped

Instructions:

1. Heat the olive oil in a large pot over medium-high heat. Add the garlic, onion, carrots, celery, and potatoes. Cook until the vegetables are tender, about 5 minutes.
2. Add the green beans, basil, oregano, thyme, and vegetable broth. Increase the heat to high and bring to a boil.
3. Reduce the heat to medium-low and add the tomatoes and orzo. Simmer for 15 minutes.
4. Add salt and pepper to taste, then stir in the fresh parsley. Serve warm.

Nutrition Information (per serving):
Calories: 170, Total Fat: 4g, Sodium: 635mg, Carbohydrates: 27g, Protein: 5g.

89. Cauliflower and Kale Minestrone Soup

Enjoy this nutritious and hearty Minestrone Soup that combines two of the trendiest vegetables out there—cauliflower and kale! This filling soup is packed with flavor and can be put together in 30 minutes. Serve it with a sprinkle of Parmesan cheese for an added savory flavor.

Serving: 8 | Preparation Time: 10 minutes | Ready Time: 30 minutes

Ingredients:
- 2 tablespoons olive oil
- 1 small yellow onion, diced
- 4 cloves garlic, minced
- 2 carrots, peeled and diced
- 2 celery stalks, diced
- 6 cups vegetable broth
- 1 tablespoon tomato paste
- 1 teaspoon dried oregano
- 1/2 teaspoon dried thyme
- 1/4 teaspoon red pepper flakes
- 1 (15-ounce) can white beans, drained and rinsed
- 2 cups cauliflower, florets
- 1 cup kale, chopped
- 1/2 teaspoon kosher salt, plus more to taste
- 1/4 teaspoon freshly ground black pepper
- 1/4 cup freshly grated Parmesan cheese, for serving

Instructions:
1. Heat the olive oil in a large soup pot over medium heat. Add the onion and garlic to the pot and cook until softened, about 5 minutes.
2. Add the carrots and celery to the pot and cook until softened, about 5 minutes.
3. Add the vegetable broth, tomato paste, oregano, thyme, and red pepper flakes to the pot and bring to a boil.
4. Once boiling, add the white beans, cauliflower, and kale to the pot. Reduce the heat to low and cook for 10 minutes.
5. Add the salt and pepper and adjust the seasoning to your preference.
6. Serve the minestrone soup in bowls with a sprinkle of Parmesan cheese.

Nutrition Information:
Serving Size: 1 cup • Calories: 150 • Fat: 4.5g • Carbs: 19g • Fiber: 4g • Protein: 5g

90. Tomato and Zucchini Minestrone Soup

Tomato and Zucchini Minestrone Soup is a hearty and healthy vegetable soup that comes together quickly and easily on the stovetop. It's vegan, gluten-free, and packed with flavor.

Serving: 4 | Preparation Time: 15 minutes | Ready Time: 20 minutes

Ingredients:
- 1 tablespoon olive oil
- 1 onion, diced
- 3 cloves garlic, minced
- 2 carrots, diced
- 2 celery stalks, diced
- 2 small zucchinis, diced
- 1/2 teaspoon dried oregano
- 1/2 teaspoon dried thyme
- 2 (28 oz) cans crushed or diced tomatoes
- 2 (14.5 oz) cans vegetable broth
- 1 (15 oz) can white beans, drained and rinsed
- 2 cups kale, chopped
- Salt and pepper, to taste

Instructions:
1. Heat the olive oil in a large pot over medium-high heat.
2. Add the onion, garlic, carrots, and celery and cook, stirring, until the vegetables are softened, about 5 minutes.
3. Add the zucchini, oregano, and thyme and cook for another 2 minutes.
4. Add the tomatoes, vegetable broth, and white beans and bring to a boil.
5. Reduce the heat and simmer for 10 minutes.
6. Add the kale and simmer for another 5 minutes.
7. Season with salt and pepper to taste.

Nutrition Information:
Calories: 250, Total Fat: 4.5g, Cholesterol: 0, Sodium: 1380mg, Total carbs: 41g, Dietary Fiber: 8.5g, Sugar: 10g, Protein: 10g

91. Bacon and Pea Minestrone Soup

Bacon and pea minestrone soup is a hearty and savory soup that everyone is sure to enjoy. This simple, rustic Italian-style soup will fill your kitchen with delicious scents and fill your bellies with warmth and flavor.

Serving: 8 | Preparation Time: 15 minutes | Ready Time: 45 minutes

Ingredients:
- 2 tablespoons of olive oil
- 8 slices of thick-cut bacon, diced
- 1 large onion, chopped
- 4 cloves of garlic, minced
- 2 large carrots, peeled and diced
- 2 stalks of celery, diced
- 1 teaspoon of dried oregano
- Salt and pepper to taste
- 1/2 teaspoon of dried thyme
- One 16-ounce bag of frozen green peas
- 8 cups of chicken or vegetable broth
- 2 cups of small pasta
- 3 tablespoons of minced fresh parsley
- Grated parmesan cheese (optional)

Instructions:
1. Heat the olive oil in a large pot over medium heat.
2. Add in the bacon and cook until crispy, about 8 to 10 minutes.
3. Remove the bacon pieces with a slotted spoon, leaving the rendered fat in the pot.
4. Add in the onions, garlic, carrots, and celery, and cook until softened, about 6 to 8 minutes.
5. Add in the oregano, salt and pepper, and thyme, and stir to combine.
6. Add in the peas, broth, and pasta, and bring to a simmer.
7. Cook for 15 to 20 minutes, or until the pasta is cooked through.
8. Stir in the chopped parsley, and the bacon pieces.
9. Serve the minestrone soup with sprinkled parmesan cheese (optional).

Nutrition Information (per serving):

Calories: 118, Protein: 6 g, Fat: 6 g, Carbs: 10 g, Sodium: 277 mg, Sugar: 1 g

92. Cannellini Bean and Artichoke Minestrone Soup

This hearty Cannellini Bean and Artichoke Minestrone Soup is a delicious and easy-to-make meal packed with healthy ingredients. It is perfect for a mid-week dinner or as a comforting lunch on a cold winter day.

Serving: 6-8 | Preparation Time: 10 minutes | Ready Time: 40 minutes

Ingredients:
- 1 tablespoon of olive oil
- 1 pound of Italian sausage, casing removed
- 1 large yellow onion, chopped
- 3 cloves of garlic, minced
- 3 medium carrots, diced
- 1 small zucchini, diced
- 2 cans of cannellini beans, rinsed and drained
- 2 cans of diced tomatoes
- 5 cups of vegetable broth
- 1/4 teaspoon of red pepper flakes
- 1 teaspoon of dried oregano
- 1/2 cup of whole artichoke hearts, drained
- 1/4 cup of fresh basil, chopped

Instruction:
1. In a large pot, heat the olive oil over medium-high heat.
2. Add the Italian sausage and cook for about 3-4 minutes, breaking up into small pieces as it cooks.
3. Add the onion, garlic, carrots, and zucchini and cook for an additional 5 minutes until the vegetables are softened.
4. Add the cannellini beans, diced tomatoes, vegetable broth, red pepper flakes, and oregano and bring to a boil.
5. Reduce the heat to low and let simmer for 20 minutes.

6. Add the artichoke hearts and fresh basil and cook for an additional 5 minutes.
7. Serve and enjoy!

Nutrition Information:
Calories: 223, Total Fat: 9.6g, Cholesterol: 20mg, Sodium: 946mg, Carbohydrates: 24.1g, Protein: 11.5g

93. Mediterranean-Style Minestrone Soup

This delicious Mediterranean-Style Minestrone Soup is the perfect combination of a variety of flavors, veggies, and protein-packed beans. It's a hearty, nutritious, and satisfying meal that comes together in under an hour.

Serving: 4-6 | Preparation Time: 15 minutes | Ready Time: 45 minutes

Ingredients:
-1 tablespoon olive oil
-1 cup diced onion
-2 cloves garlic, minced
-2 cups diced carrots
-2 cups diced potatoes
-1 cup diced zucchini
-2 teaspoons dried oregano
-1 teaspoon dried basil
-1/2 teaspoon dried thyme
-1/2 teaspoon salt
-1/4 teaspoon black pepper
-6 cups vegetable broth
-One 14-ounce can drained and rinsed cannellini beans
-One 14-ounce can drained and rinsed kidney beans
-One 14-ounce can diced fire-roasted tomatoes
-2 cups fresh spinach

Instruction:
1. Heat the oil in a large Dutch oven or stockpot over medium heat.
2. Add the onion and cook for about 5 minutes, until soft.

3. Add the garlic and cook for 1 minute, stirring frequently.
4. Add the carrots, potatoes, zucchini, oregano, basil, thyme, salt, and pepper. Cook for 5 minutes, stirring occasionally.
5. Add the broth, beans, and tomatoes. Increase the heat to high and bring to a boil.
6. Reduce the heat to low, cover, and simmer for 30 minutes.
7. Stir in the spinach, cover, and cook for 5 more minutes.
8. Taste and adjust seasoning as needed.

Nutrition Information:
per serving: 212 calories, 5.4 g fat, 32.4 g carbohydrates, 9.4 g protein, 8.4 g fiber, 680 mg sodium

94. Mushroom and Barley Minestrone Soup

Mushroom and Barley Minestrone Soup is a hearty, flavorful soup recipe perfect for fall and winter. This soup is packed with vegetables and pearl barley and also includes bacon for an added depth of flavor.

Serving: 8-10 | Preparation Time: 20 mins | Ready Time: 60 mins

Ingredients:
- 4 slices bacon, diced
- 1 onion, diced
- 1 celery stalk, diced
- 2 carrots, diced
- 3 cloves garlic, minced
- 16 oz cremini mushrooms, sliced
- 1 teaspoon dried thyme
- 1 teaspoon dried oregano
- 8-16 oz vegetable broth
- 28 oz canned diced tomatoes, no salt added
- 1/2 cup barley
- 2 zucchini, diced
- 2 cups fresh spinach
- 1 cup cooked white beans

— salt and pepper, to taste

Instructions:
1. Begin by heating a large Dutch oven over medium heat and add the bacon pieces. Cook until crispy and remove from the pan, leaving the fats in the pan.
2. To the bacon fats, add the diced onion, celery, and carrot. Cook until softened, about 3-4 minutes. Add in the garlic and mushrooms, and cook until the mushrooms are softened, about 5 minutes.
3. Add the thyme and oregano, stir together, and cook for 30 seconds until fragrant.
4. Add in the broth, diced tomatoes, and barley. Bring to a simmer and cook for 20 minutes until the barley is cooked.
5. Add in the diced zucchini, spinach, and cooked white beans. Stir together, season with salt and pepper, and cook for 5 minutes until everything is heated through.
6. Serve with bacon pieces and enjoy.

Nutrition Information (per serving):
Calories: 248; Fat: 2g; Saturated fat: 0.5g; Cholesterol: 8mg; Sodium: 284mg; Carbohydrates: 46g; Fiber: 8.6g; Sugar: 8.5g; Protein: 11g

95. Butternut Squash and Farro Minestrone Soup

Butternut Squash and Farro Minestrone Soup is a hearty vegetable-packed soup with nutritious and warming ingredients. A delicious and nourishing meal perfect for any time of the year.

Serving: 6 | Preparation Time: 15 minutes | Ready Time: 1 hour

Ingredients:
- 2 tablespoons olive oil
- 1 yellow onion, diced
- 2 cloves garlic, minced
- 2 carrots, shredded
- 2 stalks celery, diced
- 7-8 cups vegetable broth
- 1 can diced tomatoes

- 2 cups butternut squash, diced
- 1 cup dry farro
- 2 cups kale, chopped
- 1/2 teaspoon dried oregano
- 1 teaspoon sea salt
- Freshly ground black pepper, to taste

Instructions:
1. Heat the oil in a large pot over medium heat.
2. Add onion and garlic, sauté until onion is lightly browned.
3. Add carrots, celery, and sauté for another few minutes.
4. Add broth, tomatoes, butternut squash, farro, and bring to a boil.
5. Reduce heat to low and let soup simmer, covered, for 30 minutes.
6. Add kale, oregano, salt, and pepper, simmer for another 10 minutes.
7. Serve warm and enjoy!

Nutrition Information:
Per serving (6 servings): Calories: 185, Total Fat: 5.8g, Saturated Fat: 0.8g, Trans Fat: 0g, Sodium: 746mg, Total Carbohydrates: 29.7g, Dietary Fiber: 7.7g, Sugars: 7.7g, Protein: 7.5g.

96. Italian Wedding-Style Minestrone Soup

This Italian Wedding-Style Minestrone Soup is a hearty and flavorful soup that is sure to become an instant family favorite. It's brimming with colorful vegetables and made with an Italian-style broth. Perfect for a weeknight family meal or as a standout soup course for entertaining, this Italian Wedding-Style Minestrone Soup is sure to please.

Serving: 6-8 | Preparation Time: 20 minutes | Ready Time: 40 minutes

Ingredients:
- 2 tablespoons olive oil
- 1 sweet onion, chopped
- 3 cloves garlic, minced
- 2 carrots, peeled and diced
- 1 large zucchini, diced
- 1 cup celery, diced

- 3 tablespoons tomato paste
- 4 cups vegetable broth
- 1 (15-oz.) can white kidney beans, drained and rinsed
- 1 (15-oz.) can diced tomatoes
- 1 1/2 cups small shell pasta
- 1 teaspoon dried oregano
- 1 teaspoon dried basil
- 1/4 teaspoon freshly ground black pepper
- 2 tablespoons freshly chopped parsley

Instructions:

1. Heat the oil in a large stockpot over medium heat. Add the onions and garlic and cook until softened and fragrant, about 5 minutes.
2. Add the carrots, zucchini, and celery and cook, stirring occasionally, for another 5 minutes.
3. Stir in the tomato paste and cook for 1 minute.
4. Pour in the broth, beans, tomatoes, pasta and all the spices. Bring to a boil, lower heat, and simmer for 20 minutes, stirring occasionally.
5. Serve topped with fresh parsley.

Nutrition Information:

Per serving: Calories 145, Carbohydrates 20.3g, Protein 6.3g, Fat 4.7g, Saturated Fat 0.7g, Sodium 295mg, Dietary Fiber 3g.

97. Sausage and Potato Minestrone Soup

Sausage and Potato Minestrone Soup is a hearty Italian-style soup that is sure to please the whole family. Loaded with potatoes, pork sausage, and mixed vegetables, this flavorful soup is sure to become a go-to favorite.

Serving: 8-10 | Preparation Time: 10 minutes | Ready Time: 45 minutes

Ingredients:

- 2 tablespoons olive oil
- 1 pound Italian pork sausage
- 1 onion, diced
- 2 carrots, diced

- 2 stalks celery, diced
- 4 cloves garlic, minced
- 8 cups chicken broth
- 2 Yukon gold potatoes, cubed
- 2 (14.5 ounce) cans diced tomatoes
- 1 (15 ounce) can white beans, drained and rinsed
- 2 zucchini, chopped
- 2 sprigs fresh thyme
- 2 teaspoons Italian seasoning
- Salt and black pepper, to taste

Instructions:
1. Heat the olive oil in a large Dutch oven or pot over medium-high heat. Brown the sausage and onion until the sausage is no longer pink.
2. Add the carrots, celery, and garlic. Sauté for 5 minutes until vegetables are tender.
3. Add the chicken broth, potatoes, tomatoes, beans, zucchini and thyme. Season with Italian seasoning, salt and pepper. Bring the soup to a boil and reduce heat to medium-low. Simmer for 35 minutes or until potatoes are tender.
4. Remove the thyme sprigs and discard. Serve warm with crusty bread.

Nutrition Information: (Per Serving)
Calories: 302, Fat: 15g, Carbohydrates: 26g, Protein: 16g, Sodium: 964mg, Cholesterol: 34mg

98. Turkey and Kale Minestrone Soup

Turkey and Kale Minestrone Soup is an Italian-inspired soup that is packed with protein and is sure to satisfy any craving. This hearty soup contains a blend of ground turkey, vegetables, kale, and a variety of spices. The best part about this dish is that it's healthy and can easily be made in the comfort of your own kitchen.

Serving: 6 | Preparation Time: 15 minutes | Ready Time: 45 minutes

Ingredients:
- 1 tablespoon olive oil

- 1 Cup diced onion
- 2 cloves garlic, minced
- 1 pound ground turkey
- 2 tablespoons tomato paste
- 2 cups chicken broth
- 2 cups diced potatoes
- 1 (14-ounce) can diced tomatoes
- 1 cup chopped carrots
- 1 cup chopped celery
- 1 teaspoon oregano
- 1/2 teaspoon thyme
- 1 cup canned white beans, drained and rinsed
- 1/2 cup chopped kale
- Salt and pepper, to taste

Instructions:
1. Heat olive oil in a large pot over medium-high heat. Add the onion and garlic and cook for 3 minutes, stirring occasionally.
2. Add the ground turkey and cook for 6 minutes, stirring and breaking apart the meat.
3. Add the tomato paste, chicken broth, potatoes, tomatoes, carrots, celery, oregano, and thyme. Bring to a boil, then reduce heat and simmer uncovered for 25 minutes.
4. Add the white beans and kale and simmer for an additional 10 minutes.
5. Season with salt and pepper, to taste. Serve warm.

Nutrition Information:
Calories: 163 kcal, Carbohydrates: 16 g, Protein: 15 g, Fat: 5 g, Saturated Fat: 1 g, Cholesterol: 33 mg, Sodium: 370 mg, Potassium: 586 mg, Fiber: 5 g, Sugar: 3 g, Vitamin A: 3736 IU, Vitamin C: 31 mg, Calcium: 43 mg, Iron: 3 mg.

CONCLUSION

Minestrone soup has been an all-time favorite side or main dish around the world for generations. The 99 Delicious Minestrone Soup Recipes: A Collection of Hearty Soups for Every Occasion book provides a vast array of preparation techniques and ingredients to make minestrone soup, tailored to every taste and situation. With this collection, the options for making a delicious and nutritious minestrone soup are limitless.

From traditional Italian flavors to innovative and adventurous combinations, this cookbook has something special for everyone. Whether it's a vegan medley, a seafood version, or an inventive take on an old classic - there is bound to be something to please all tasters. Both the beginner and the advanced cook will find recipes suitable to their level of skill and experience. Not to mention, the collection is complete with money-saving tips to ensure all recipes are affordable and easy on the budget.

For home cooks, chefs, and all who love a delicious and healthy soup, this cookbook is invaluable for creating flavorful and nutritious minestrone soup. Whether you're looking for a quick, easy dinner for two or a big bowl of warmth for a big crowd, the options are ample. And no matter what the occasion, your soup will be sure to be memorable and hassle-free.

For satisfying and nourishing minestrone soup recipes, look no further than the 99 Delicious Minestrone Soup Recipes: A Collection of Hearty Soups for Every Occasion. With such a wide and creative selection, it's easy to see why this cookbook should be a staple in every home. Enjoy deliciously hearty soups for any occasion every time.